BULLET PROOF
PROOF
MARRIAGE

BULLET PROOF MARRIAGE

Your shield against divorce

RENATO&
CRISTIANE
CARDOSO

To all couples who value their marriage enough to bullet-proof it. And to smart singles who know that prevention is better than the cure.

CONTENTS

PART II
EMOTION VS. REASON

PART III
TAKING MARRIAGE APART
AND PUTTING IT BACK TOGETHER

PART IV
BULLETPROOFING IT

PREFACE

"Defence! Defence!"

As you read this preface, you would probably expect references to basketball, a sport that has brought me achievement, struggle, joy, conflict and reward. Instead, I would like to speak about another area of my life that has also brought achievement, struggle, joy, conflict and reward, but much deeper and more meaningful: my marriage.

Cristina and I have been married for over thirty years, and have known each other for nearly four decades. I know this sounds like a cliché, but I cannot help it, and I am sure you will agree: it seems like we've always been together. Imagine all the things that can happen in a lifetime —sunny days and perfect weather, but also rainy days and storms. It takes a well-grounded relationship to resist the stormy winds of life.

Forty years ago, when I was more naïve, I would have said that every problem in a marriage could be solved with love. Obviously, it is a key element to any relationship—no couple can stay together and be happy without love—but I can assure you that there are many more aspects to marriage.

Only this can explain my wife, Cristina, giving up on her college degree only three months before graduation, and moving to Europe with me where I started playing six months after our wedding. In those first weeks, she supported both of us financially, when the team I was playing on started the season on the wrong foot. No matter how much I had to train or concentrate on my game, Cristina never dropped the ball at home. Without her, I would have given up. With her, I returned home a champion a few years later.

In basketball (okay, I am talking about basketball after all), no self-respecting team will get results unless they work as a team. One minute you're scoring a point and the next you're getting a rebound. In the United States, fans shout, "Defence! Defence!" and I've realised that marriage is exactly the same. When we love, not only do we advance, progress and conquer, we also protect our spouse and relationship. I've turned down so many requests from fans out of respect for Cristina. I was determined to spare her the embarrassment, and preserve our unity, love, and our relationship.

This is why I was thrilled with the request to write the preface of Renato and Cristiane Cardoso's book. I've read a few books on marriage and heard of others, but this is the first time that I've found one that goes to the heart of the issue: bulletproofing your marriage. Bullet-proofing is just that—creating defences that will block anything that would potentially jeopardise the relationship. This includes external and internal attacks like nit-picking, crises (they always appear), not knowing how to lovingly give in/stand your ground, inability to adapt to each other's strengths and defects, blackmailing, emotional games... the list goes on and on.

Renato and Cristiane learned these things after many years of couple's counselling, but their best training was the school of life. This is where they discovered the power of bulletproofing their marriage, which is stronger and more solid when it is based on Christian principles and values. And now they share these experiences and guidance in this book. It is a spectacular opportunity for both those who think that their marriage is vulnerable and needs to be shielded, and for those who have bulletproofed their marriage and know the importance of providing continual protection. Read it and bulletproof your marriage too.

Oscar Schmidt

Hall of Famer and Brazil's all-time
greatest basketball player, married to Cristina
and father of Felipe and Stephanie

INTRODUCTION

People don't get married out of hate. I have never heard of anyone asking for a person's hand in marriage by saying, "I hate you! Will you marry me?" People marry for love. Despite that, divorce rates continue to rise each year. In some countries, such as the U.S., half of all marriages end in divorce. Europe is following suit: 2010 figures show that one couple divorce for every two couples that get married. If the rising trend continues, by 2025 there will be more divorces than marriages. People are so scared by this rate of failure that many are shunning marriage altogether. In the UK for example, for the first time in history, most babies will be born out of wedlock by 2016. We are going from bad to worse.

This scenario is being repeated in most parts of the world: Latin and Central America, Africa, Oceania and Asia. It shows that the "love" that binds people together has not been enough to maintain a strong marriage. Scary, isn't it? Just imagine: the love that you have for each other may not be enough in times of a marriage crisis!

The problem is not a lack of love, but a lack of tools to solve the problems that come along with living together. People get married with virtually no ability to solve problems that arise with married life. For some reason, this is not taught anywhere—at least, not in the clear, practical way it needs to be. Back in the old days, these teachings came from parents. When marriages were solid and exemplary, children looked to their parents as models of how to behave in a relationship. Nowadays, parents are often an example of what not to do...

We have another big problem: Ignorance of the true meaning of love. I have often heard many frustrated husbands and wives say, "We've fallen out of love. I no longer feel what I felt for him/her." Others say that their marriage was a mistake, they married the wrong person, they got married too soon, or they were forced into marriage because of a particular circumstance, like an unplanned pregnancy. The truth is, more often than not, married people are unhappy because of *what they are doing wrong*, not because *they married the wrong person*. People do so many wrong things in their relationships. They accumulate problems without ever solving them, which leads to a suffocated, crushed and helpless love—that is, if it isn't killed before it's even born. Good feelings end up giving way to anger, indifference and even hatred.

But you can salvage your love, and even learn to love someone you have never loved. Pay close attention to what I just said: You can learn to love. The first step is understanding that the only way to love a person is to get to know them on a deeper level.

Many make the mistake of viewing love as a feeling. It is correct to say that love produces good feelings, but it is not a feeling. When you meet a person for the first time and feel something good for them, but then do not learn how to love them for who they are, that "love at first sight" will not last very long. Love is not felt. Love is knowing the other person, admiring everything you learn about them, and seeing their flaws in a positive light. We can learn to love anyone or anything, if we dedicate ourselves to it.

For example, let's take a look at Dian Fossey. The epitaph on her gravestone reads: "No one loved gorillas more". Dian was an American zoologist, who was known and respected for her studies of gorillas in

Central Africa. Dian lived among the mountain gorillas of Rwanda for many years, until poachers murdered her. She lived in a log cabin, in primitive conditions, and dedicated more than 18 years of her life to these animals, whom she loved more than anything in life. How did Dian's love for gorillas begin?

At 31, when she went on an African safari, Dian had her first encounter with gorillas and the studies of conservationists who worked for the preservation of the primates. This was when she began learning more about this species, their behaviour, how they communicate, their habits, their diet, their threat of extinction, and much more. Dian is credited for debunking the negative reputation that gorillas gained after the King Kong movie depicted them as aggressive and wild animals. Her studies showed that in reality, these animals are "dignified, highly social, gentle giants, with individual personalities and strong family relationships"—putting them well ahead of many men...

My point is that she *learned* to love gorillas. Anyone who loves someone or something, initiates that love by gaining knowledge about the object of their love. Some people love animals, others love stars and celestial bodies, others love toy soldiers, and still others love architecture... But the love of each one sprang from studying, learning and becoming knowledgeable about what or whom they loved. Nobody loves what they do not know.

Unfortunately, many couples never learned to love each other. A feeling, passion or some other influence brought them together, but they never learned how to study or explore each other, or discover what makes them happy. When you do not know another person it is impossible to love them because you do not know what pleases or annoys them, their dreams and struggles, or how they think. In such ignorance, you will make many mistakes in your relationship and so cause many problems. These problems will cause you to withdraw, even though you are married and were in love at one time.

If you have been wondering:

- Do I still love my husband/wife?
- Did I marry the wrong person?
- Why is my partner so cold to me?
- Why do we love each other but can't stay together?
- How can I make sure my marriage lasts?
- How can I live with a person who is so difficult?
- Why do our problems go away, but then come back worse than before?
- Is my marriage always going to be about hardships, or will I find happiness one day?

Cheer up! You will learn how to love intelligently and how to be happy with your spouse, even if he (or she) acts like King Kong...

THE AUTHORS

Cristiane and I got married in 1991 and have an adopted son. I came from a broken home, which was ruined by infidelity and divorce. My parents were the reason for the one-eighty in my life when I was only 13. At the time, a series of events caused their separation, which was very traumatic for me. I felt like the whole world was crumbling down around me.

My father was my hero, but when I learned that he had had an affair, despair came over me. I began questioning why this was happening. I wanted death. Driven by this pain, I found faith and turned to the Lord Jesus. Later, this faith also reached my parents and after many years of suffering, their lives too were restored. I did not learn a religious faith, but one that I was able to use to solve problems. This is why I decided to dedicate my life to sharing what I have learned with others, so that they will be able to overcome their difficulties as well. I could not keep to myself those insights which literally saved my life and my parents' lives.

Later, I married Cristiane. Since she was a pastor's daughter, we shared the same goals. On the surface, we had everything for a trouble-free marriage, but it was not that easy. We faced various problems, many of which we will discuss in this book.

Strengthening marriages, educating couples and singles, and fighting for fewer marriages to end in divorce, became a mission in my life. Today I know that the pain I felt during my teenage years when my parents separated, and later in my marriage, could have been avoided. If my parents had access to the information you will have in this book, they would not have gone through all the hardships they did. If Cristiane and I knew all the things you are about to read in this book before we got married, we would not have caused each other to suffer.

Unfortunately, people suffer because of a lack of knowledge. Nowadays there are schools for all kinds of training, but not for marriage. Even among Christians, there are plenty of theories about love, dating and marriage, but when the time comes to put these things into practice, people generally do not know what to do. Useful relationship skills and marriage education are rare. So here are two reasons why we dedicate ourselves to passing on this knowledge to other couples: (1) for dating couples and newlyweds to avoid making mistakes that can jeopardise the future of their relationship, and (2) for those who are already in a troubled marriage to learn how to solve problems and live together happily.

Cristiane and I speak from personal experience in our marriage, and from years of counselling other couples. As part of our work across four continents, we have counselled thousands of couples, from teenagers to sexagenarians (never older; it seems that couples in their 70s realise that life is too short to be fighting all the time...), and due to high demand, our work with couples has increased in recent years.

In late 2007, our work took us to Texas in the United States. This is where the concept of The Bulletproof Marriage course evolved which resulted in this book. We felt compelled to share our experiences there because of this alarming fact: Out of every ten marriages, almost six end in divorce.

The American couples that came to us for counselling had been through multiple relationships and continued to have problems. Many were already in their third, fourth, even fifth marriage, and had clearly not learned anything from their previous relationships. We felt an obligation to help them, to pass on what we had learned. The results helped us to realise that although our experiences and lessons were nothing new, they had a transforming effect in the lives of many couples.

I believe this is due to the unique combination of factors that Cris and I have put together: (1) personal experience, (2) experiences we have gained from counselling thousands of couples across four continents, and (3) the use of spiritual intelligence. Let me briefly explain the third factor.

Marriage was God's idea. He decided that man and woman should be "one flesh". Furthermore, the Bible says "God is love[1]". So if two people trying to live as one want to function well, it is only smart to return to the origins, where it all began, and to the Source of love. This is why our lessons are based on the intelligence of God—on those things that He determined would work. This does not mean that the objective of this book is to convert you to Christ, if you are not a Christian. Nor will we be referring to the Bible throughout the book, though at times it will be inevitable. However, I must say: Without the principles established by God as the foundation for a good marriage, your efforts will be in vain. We have noticed that couples that have embraced this fact are the happiest and the most successful in their efforts to restore and maintain their marriages.

An additional factor in the great success of our teachings is that we focus our help on two main points: Solving problems and preventing them from happening again. Most marital problems are recurring. Therefore, it is not enough for you to know how to solve the problems

---

[1] John 4.8

 22

you are now having, you need to cut the problem at its root so it does not come back again in the future.

We are certain that if you read this book with an open mind and are willing to at least try to apply the tools we teach you, you will have a strong and happy marriage. Remember: Practice makes perfect.

P.S. There are tasks at the end of some chapters, so you can apply what you have learned. Do not underestimate the power of these exercises. We believe that if you are reading this book, it's because you want to see results, but they will only come when you put what you have learned to the test. This is so serious that we invite you to make your efforts public. If you are part of a social network, share the tasks that you are performing so that others can motivate you throughout your journey. Why not start now? Post your comments on our page facebook. com/BulletproofMarriage so we can track your progress (we have also posted videos on this page to help you with your tasks... check them out!). On Twitter, make sure you tweet us @BulletproofMate and add the hashtag *#Bulletproofmarriage* (Facebook also now accepts hashtags).

/BulletproofMarriage

Post: Today, I begin to bulletproof my marriage.
#Bulletproofmarriage

@BulletproofMate

Tweet: Today, I begin to bulletproof my marriage.
#Bulletproofmarriage
@BulletproofMate

PART I

UNDERSTANDING MARRIAGE

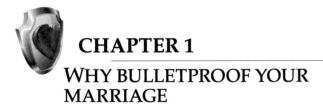

CHAPTER 1
WHY BULLETPROOF YOUR MARRIAGE

Concerned about the rising rate of divorce, some Mexico City lawmakers are proposing a new law: Renewable marriage contracts. They believe they have found the perfect solution for the crises of marital breakup, infidelity and divorce. Every two years, married couples would have the option to re-evaluate their relationship and choose whether to remain together and renew their contract or give up and go their separate ways. In addition to signing a temporary contract, the proposal suggests that bride and groom protect themselves from potential divorce. Before marriage, they would have to decide who will have custody of the children and how much will be paid in child support in case there is a break-up. The proposal, which is now in Congress, has received broad support from Mexicans, who want to end the high cost of divorce and alimony. After all, marriage statistics in Mexico City are bleak: Five out of ten marriages end in divorce.

If the law is passed, conversations like this may become commonplace between classmates in school:

—Hey, where are you going over the school holidays? (*asks a boy of his friend*)

—Well, that depends. If my dad renews the contract with my mum at the end of the year, we'll probably go to Disneyland. If not, I'll have to see which one of them wants me, and since my last few report cards have been pretty bad, they'll probably send me to my grandma's...

I don't want to be the bearer of bad news, but here's a fact: Marriage as an institution is under heavy attack from various elements in society. This Mexican proposal is a symptom of governments' attempts to cope with high divorce rates. And this is not limited to Mexico. I don't know of a single country, culture or society in the world where marriage is getting stronger, not even in traditional cultures where religion is valued. In the United States, which dictates the cultural trends for the rest of the world, most babies born to women under the age of 30 are born out of wedlock. Some renowned American sociologists have even argued that father figures are not essential in families.

Can you see where we're headed?

Even in places where divorce rates are lower, the numbers do not always reflect what's actually happening: Fewer people are getting married while increasing numbers are opting for "cohabitation".

When these couples do separate, it does not count statistically as a divorce. And many who remain in their relationships do so for lack of alternatives or because of religious pressure, but confess to being unhappy.

The harsh reality of the situation makes me wonder what things will be like in five, ten or twenty years. Will the extinction of marriage be complete? Will people still believe in "till death do us part"? Will the concepts of marital faithfulness and loyalty to a single person be relegated to museums and historical documentaries?

Here's a warning for those who have not yet woken up: *Forces in society are conspiring against marriage and the family, and these attacks are only increasing.*

THE METAMORPHOSIS OF MARRIAGE

The media (movies, TV, the Internet, books, newspapers), cultural norms, politics, laws, celebrities, schools and universities—all of society's major centres of influence—are becoming, or have already become, anti-marriage.

What does this mean?

- There will be a sizeable decrease in the number of marriages
- Cohabitation will become more and more common—inferring that long-term, absolute commitment is impossible
- Infidelity and affairs will increase (yes, even more) and become more and more forgivable
- Casual dating outside a relationship, with sex as the sole purpose, will be acceptable
- Men and women will become even more predatory
- Women will view men as non-essential, and will grow even more independent
- Women will bounce between no longer believing in love (or men) and the search for happiness at the expense of their own sense of worth

Note: All of the above are ALREADY happening in today's society. It's the metamorphosis of marriage, and time will only speed up this process.

You may not be able to change what's happening around the world, but within your own world, inside your marriage, you can and must. This is not a question of whether or not your relationship will come under attack, but when. The question is: Will you know how to protect it from these attacks when they come—that is, if it's not already under attack?

MARRIAGE IN THE FACEBOOK ERA

The Internet, social networks, SMS, chat rooms, easy access to pornography, an anti-marriage culture, easy divorces and the advancement of women in society, are a few of the recent phenomena affecting couples in the 21st century, and many are not prepared to handle these new challenges. Couples today are faced with a new reality, a world that their parents never knew, in fact, no generation has ever known.

Ask your grandmother how she would have known her husband was having an affair, and she'll say, "lipstick stains on his shirt" or "another woman's perfume". Today, it is so much easier to have an affair behind your partner's back.

Mark Zuckerberg, the creator of Facebook, has been billed as one of the greatest destroyers of homes in Great Britain. According to a study published by Divorce-Online, a website that specialises in divorces, Facebook is cited as the reason for one in every three divorces in the country. Close to 1,700 of the 5,000 cases mentioned that inappropriate messages to the opposite sex and comments from ex-girlfriends on Facebook were the cause of their marital problems. In the U.S., the American Academy of Matrimonial Lawyers released an article stating that in 2011, Facebook is cited in one of every five divorces.

To have a better idea of where things are heading, get this: a new kind of social network has been rapidly gaining ground in the online world. They have been labelled "adultery networks" and target married people who "live in a marriage without sex and want to find others in the same situation". Committed men and women are offered a "discreet way of having an affair". One such site claims over 15 million users spread over the U.S., the UK and a handful of other countries. It offers a private e-mail account and an innocent sounding name on the credit card bill—all in an attempt to facilitate casual sex encounters that leave no trail for the betrayed partner to follow. One slogan reads: "An affair can save a marriage."

Outrageous, right? You ain't seen nothing yet.

What's the fastest growing business in the world, with greater turn-over than Google, Apple, Amazon, Netflix, eBay, Microsoft and Yahoo put together? Porn. In 2006, this industry brought in US$97 billion. More porn movies are made throughout the world than any other cat-egory, by far. This translates to an average of about 37 movies per day, or more than 13,500 per year. The U.S. is the largest producer of this genre of movie. English-speaking countries are responsible for 95% of all porn web pages on the Internet. One study reported that seven out of ten men aged 18 to 34 visit pornographic websites on the Internet. Women, once uncomfortable with this type of behaviour, have been increasingly seeking out porn in order to please their partners.

"But thank God we're Christians and this doesn't affect us." Don't be too fast to jump to conclusions.

A survey of Christians in the U.S. revealed that 50% of men and 20% of women who attend church were addicted to pornography. Another survey held solely among pastors revealed that 54% of them had seen pornography within the last 12 months, and 30% within the 30 days preceding the survey.

Is anyone immune?

MAN VS. WOMAN – THE FINAL BATTLE

For the first time in the history of the male species, men are feeling displaced and lost in their marriages. With the advancement of women in practically every facet of society, they have become competitors to men and moved on from the traditional role of helpers. Men—who used to be the sole hunters, providers and protectors of the family—now view their role as shared with, and often taken over by women. Women have become hunters too.

Most women in a relationship work and contribute to the family's income. In some cases, a wife earns more than her husband, a trend that is likely to increase, since university enrolment among women is higher than men in many countries of the world.

What effect does this have on marriage? Here are a few examples: Women have become more independent than men. Women are less tolerant of men's flaws. Wives are making decisions without their husbands' input, causing serious disagreement. In an attempt to please women, men have become more sensitive. Men have taken a backseat in their marriages. Husbands feel disrespected by their wives, and at times even disposable. In other words, women have become more like men, and men have become more like women—a complete mess and confusion of their roles.

But women are not advancing and competing with men only in the workplace. A study performed by the University of São Paulo revealed a worrying statistic for married men. Extramarital affairs among women are growing at an alarming rate, and the younger they are, the more they cheat. Of the 8,200 women surveyed in ten cities throughout Brazil, only 22% of women over 70 years of age confessed to having had some kind of extramarital affair. The rate rises to 35% for women between 41 and 50 years of age and reaches a peak of 49.5% between 18 and 25 years of age. This means that half of all young married women today betray their husbands. This trend can be be reliably extrapolated to other countries. As women have emerged from the simple stay-at-home-mother role to a more active role in society, college, the workplace, etc. they are ideally positioned for infidelity.

Add to this the steady stream of conscious and subconscious attacks by the media levelled at the foundation of marriage: reality TV, movies, magazines, blogs, news, fashion, music... Each one is a pointed gun firing round after round: Why get married? A piece of paper isn't going to make a bit of difference... Have fun but don't get too attached... If he's not the right person, get divorced and find someone else... Male, female, it's all the same thing... There's no such thing as love, it's all an illusion...

Marriage is a prison... How could anyone put up with the same person for 20, 30 or 50 years? Marriage is old-fashioned...

Every day, a new anti-marriage argument is created.

If you value your relationship and do not want to become another statistic, bulletproofing your marriage is the key to its survival. It's time to defend and protect your most precious investment, before it's too late. Let's fight for this.

If you are genuinely committed to bulletproofing your relationship, then start to follow the advice and tasks that we recommend in this book.

TASK:

What are the greatest threats to your marriage right now? Identify these threats, and always be aware of the areas of your marriage that need the most help.

(Wait! Before noting down your task on the lines below, ask yourself if you plan to lend out or give this book to someone when you've finished with it. If so, it would not be proper for them to read your notes and know all about the struggles you are facing in your marriage...In this case, we suggest that you write down your tasks somewhere else—a notebook, diary, or computer file. Do what you think is best. I simply wanted you to think about that before you started.)

_____

_____

_____

/BulletproofMarriage

Post: I've identified
the current threats
to my marriage.
#Bulletproofmarriage

@BulletproofMate

Tweet: I've identified
the current threats to
my marriage.
#BulletproofMarriage
@BulletproofMate

CHAPTER 2
IT'S DEEPER

If I were a fly on the wall of your living room or bedroom when you and your spouse were having an argument, what would I see? Harsh words, hurtful comments, anger, irritation, interruptions, accusations, criticisms and so on. One day you disagree about the way to discipline your children, the next day about how your husband "friended" an ex-girlfriend on Facebook, the following day you disagree about how your mother-in-law interferes in your marriage. The point is, the real problem is not always what you see. The problem is deeper.

A simple example is when a husband has an addiction. His wife sees him giving in to it and thinks that that is the problem. She gets angry, criticises him, tries to talk to him and asks him to change, but nothing ever changes. Why not? Because the addiction is not the real problem. There is a root, something deeper, that is the cause of the addiction. She doesn't know what it is—perhaps neither does he—but the two of them will go around and around in circles arguing about what they see on the surface.

The visible problems are the leaves, twigs and branches of the tree, but the true causes are less apparent and more difficult to detect and understand. And yet, the only reason for visible problems to exist is the fact that there is a root that feeds them. If there were no roots, the tree would not exist.

Once you've identified the root of the problems in your relationship, you will understand why you and your partner act the way you do. The arguments about the leaves and branches will become fewer, as will the bad atmosphere that exists between you. The elimination of one bad root will result in the solution of several problems at once, permanently! This is the power behind this shift of focus. Learning to focus your attention and energy on the real problem can transform your marriage, because everything, including our behaviour, depends on how we look at things, what we look at and how we interpret what we are looking at.

Stephen Covey talks about an event in his life that taught him the importance of putting this into practice.

He recounts how one day he was quietly riding the subway, reading the newspaper. The subway car was pretty quiet and various seats were available. At one of the stops, a father entered with two very loud children and sat down next to him. The boys started running around, were loud and immediately disturbed the peace everyone had been enjoying. The father was sitting with his eyes closed and seemed not to care about anything that was happening. Covey did not understand the father's indifference, and angrily turned to him and asked why he was not doing anything to control his children. As if he had only then noticed what was happening, the father replied, "You're right, I'm sorry. We only now left the hospital. Their mother just passed away. I don't know what to do and it seems like they don't either... " Covey apologised and began to comfort the man. Immediately, all the anger he had felt for the father and children disappeared and gave way to empathy.

But what caused Covey's attitude to change? He began to look at the situation in a different light. Before he was given that information from the father, Covey watched what was happening through the lens of his own principles and values. "How can a parent allow his children to be so out of control? If they were my children..." But after receiving this new information, his view on things made a radical change. Notice how none of the people changed: The children did not stop misbehaving, and the father did not do anything to control them. Covey's perspective of the situation was the only thing that changed, and along with it, his attitude.

The same thing happens in marriage. You judge your partner, and demand that he change because you see him through the lens of your own experiences, values and concepts. But this conflict occurs when we do not understand or pay attention to what is the real cause of each particular situation. And so, one of the first steps we need to take to transform the present reality of our marriages has to do with our perspectives—how we look at things, what we look at and how we interpret what we're looking at. The challenge is knowing where to look, because the root is not always easy to identify. Let me try to help you by using another analogy.

ONE FLESH, TWO SETS OF PROBLEMS

When two people get married, they each bring into the marriage their own sets of problems and personal issues. What you don't see on the pearly wedding invitation are things like, "John Doe, porn addict, severely bullied as a kid, extremely insecure as a man, will marry Jane Doe, abused as a child, a walking time-bomb, who's ready for anything that gets her out of her parents' house."

Their past is not going to be printed on the wedding invitations—in fact, it will not be printed anywhere. And yet, no one gets married without dragging their own baggage into the relationship. For example, in the case of this couple, John and Jane, do you have any idea where this union is headed?

On your wedding day, you typically only know 10 to 20% of the person you are marrying, at best, and most of that is knowledge about his or her good side. That's because most of us do a good job of hiding our flaws when we are dating. I say "hide" not because we intentionally deceive the other person, but simply the natural process of getting someone to fall in love with you. A part of the dating process is doing all you can to make a good impression on the other person. You always wear the best clothes, think before you speak, walk away when you have flatulence, go out to eat at nice restaurants... In fact, the typical restaurant scene illustrates this point extremely well.

He'll choose a restaurant you like and you'll be seated at the table and order your food. In between admiring glances, there are compliments about your hair and clothes, and you enjoy the moment to the fullest. In the end, he pays the bill without complaining and you both leave happy.

After marriage, this scenario is a little different. Dinner will be at the kitchen table, with minimum or no decoration. He'll say something about how the potatoes are not the way he likes them. Then, for the very first time, you'll notice that he makes an annoying sound when he chews... apart from other noises that are accompanied by a not-so-pleasant odour. When you're finished, you notice that he doesn't even take his plate over to the sink, let alone offer to wash the dishes... This is when you ask yourself: "Why did I marry this thing?"

Welcome to marriage! This is the time you truly begin to get to know each other. And with this "new" knowledge comes problems.

This is why I encourage those who are dating to be transparent and open with respect to their personalities and backgrounds, in order to minimise surprises in the future. Don't allow yourself to be so charmed by your date as to assume that he or she only has a good side. Dating is when you should discover everything you can about the person you are about to marry. Things like their past, family, how they were brought up, what kind of relationship they had with their parents, etc.

Marriage is not the place or the time to be surprised. Nobody wants to find out from their husband's ex-girlfriend six months after they're married that he has a son. The honeymoon is not the time for a wife to explain that she has difficulty being intimate with her husband because she was abused as a child. The more you know about each other, the less chance there is of coming across unpleasant surprises.

We once counselled a young man who was determined to leave his wife weeks after they were married. His reason for leaving was that during their honeymoon he discovered that his wife was not a virgin, as she had led him to believe. He felt betrayed by the fact that she had kept this a secret, and had difficulty overcoming the emotional pain of knowing she had been intimate with other men. What to some would seem petty, to him was reason enough to consider divorce. It was hard to convince him to forgive her and overcome his negative emotions. They remained together, but their early years of marriage were marked by serious problems.

A person's bad past should not be an obstacle to marriage. Let whoever has no skeletons in the closet, throw the first stone... But it's crucial that we be aware of how our past can affect our present and future.

Imagine the patience and understanding required of a man whose wife was sexually abused as a child. In order to determine whether or not he's up to the task, he has to be aware of the whole picture.

When two people get married, their pasts also comes along. And their pasts will determine their behaviour within the relationship. For this reason, you cannot look only at the person you are with today, even if you have already been married for years. You have to know who this person is and what their roots are—where he came from, who she is, what circumstances and people influenced him and made him into the person he is today—and everything that contributed to this. Only then will you be able to fully understand the situation and respond effectively.

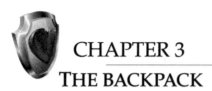

CHAPTER 3
THE BACKPACK

Imagine a bride and groom before a church altar. They are dressed for a wedding in front of all their guests. A pastor performs the ceremony. But attached to each of their backs, over her white gown and his rented tux, are large, heavy backpacks. Inside each backpack is their past, the baggage they bring into the marriage, whose contents they are about to discover: Their upbringing, what they learned from their parents, past experiences, trauma, fear of rejection, insecurity, expectations...

This is why anyone about to get married should behave like airport security: "Open your suitcase. I want to see what's inside!"

I've heard many couples say, "Your past doesn't matter to me, I only care about us and our future." Well, this sounds very romantic, but it will not stop the past from being dragged into their present relationship. Your past is a part of you; it is impossible to get rid of. But you can learn how to deal with it, whatever it is. However, if you do not know each other's past, will you know what to do when it tries to interfere in the future, after you are married?

Let us share a personal example of how this baggage affects a couple right from the beginning.

5.6 SECONDS OF FREEDOM

When Cristiane and I got married, we began to have problems because I gave her very little attention. Understandably, she became very demanding of me. Six days a week I would get up early and go to work, return late at night, tired, and bringing work home with me. On Saturday, what was supposed to be my day off, I would volunteer to go to work for at least part of the morning. Still very young and wanting to make an impression in my workplace, I knew I would have to dedicate myself.

I worked as if I were still single, forgetting that I now had a wife. I was unbalanced when it came to work and family. Cristiane stayed home most of the time, and when I came home at night, she would always ask me the same question: "How was your day?" The last thing I wanted to talk about at that point was how my day had gone, because I was exhausted. So I would give her a three-word answer: "It was good." Unsatisfied, she would insist: "Did anything interesting happen?" And I would answer with four more words: "No, it was normal." Obviously (but not so obvious to me back then), she felt excluded from my life. I only cared about food, finishing the work I had brought home and going straight to bed because I was dead tired. Add this all up and what you have is the perfect recipe for an unhappy wife.

But that was during the week. On Saturday, things got worse. My dear wife thought, "Well, at least we'll be able to go somewhere on Saturday." Poor thing. Since the most important workday of the week for me was Sunday, every single Saturday I was concerned about planning and preparing for the next day. For the few hours that remained on Saturday afternoon and night, I just wanted to rest, but she wanted to go out to a movie. And because she had put up with my lack of attention throughout the week, she was even more determined on Saturday: "Where are we going today?" "Can we see a movie?" "Let's go out for lunch." "Let's invite so-and-so to go out with us." And so I would look at her with "that face" and say: "Are you serious? Don't you understand that this is the only time I have to be at home and rest?" I viewed her as extremely annoying and felt that she did not understand me at all. My defence was: "You knew what my work hours were before we got married. This is how it's always been and now you're making it into a big deal." In reality, my days and work hours had not changed, but I had forgotten that while we were dating I would set aside time on Saturdays to go out with her. In reality, I was the one who had changed.

Cristiane Cardoso:

I was a pastor's daughter and throughout my life I was either at home or in church. When I got married at 17, it was as if until then my right wrist had been handcuffed to my father's left wrist, and there at the altar, he had unlocked the handcuffs, put them on Renato's wrist, closed them again and given him the key. By the clock, I had experienced 5.6 seconds of freedom... Of course, at the time it did not seem that way. I thought everything would change after marriage because while we were dating Renato would call me, we would go out and would spend one day of the week together. He was super romantic, wrote me love letters all the time, and made me feel like the most important girl in the world.

However, my expectations went down the drain. Soon after we got married, Renato was transferred to New York and I found myself far from my family and all of my friends. We lived an hour away from his job, which ate into even more of the little time we had together.

I wanted to follow my mother's example and be a good wife to Renato and make him very happy. I dedicated myself to our home, spent the whole day taking care of his clothes, cooked every day and always made sure to look good for him when he arrived in the evening. But this was all very difficult because I was young and had just graduated from high school. The food did not taste very good, I would iron his linen shirts three different times, and even then they didn't look right, the cleaning products burned my skin... and I thought, "Renato's coming home later and he'll appreciate all my hard work"—Nope! He didn't even notice.

Renato was my first boyfriend and everything I had ever dreamed of, but I turned my marriage into a serious mess. I was sad and began to complain, cry and be demanding—and he would insist on saying that he had always been that way and I should learn to live with it. I would have to adapt to this kind of life. The only days of the week that I was out was in church Wednesday and Friday nights. They were the most interesting days of the week! No wonder I was so eager for him to ar-rive home all the other nights—he was the only friend I had to talk to. But he did not understand my needs and was never in the mood to talk. It even got to the point that I thought my husband was no longer in love with me.

I was so inexperienced and young, had never been in any other relationship, and so everything made me suspicious. At times I would arrive at church and see Renato counselling a woman (part of his job) and would get jealous. "How can he pay so much attention to people he doesn't even know and not care about me, his wife, who does everything for him?" After making comments like this, it would be all over—my husband would shut down even more. He would give me the famous "silent treatment" that would at times last for three days! He would speak to and smile at everyone else, but when it came to me... it was as if I did not exist. Obviously, that did not help me deal with all the insecurity I had brought into our marriage. It only made it worse.

My upbringing was very different from his. My family always spoke openly about what we were feeling, no matter what was going on. And so I continued to do the same at home with Renato, but instead of getting upset with me, saying what he had to say and then returning to normal, he would say nothing, look at me annoyed and stop talking to me for days. This contrast in dealing with problems made our disagreements even worse. On top of the problems at work—the pressure and responsibility—he would come home to even more problems. Everything was new to me and I had no one to talk to, and so I wanted him to be my friend, but all I got was a frustrated husband who thought I was a nag.

When I stopped demanding his attention, I saw results. He began to do what I liked and what pleased me, without me even asking. Today we talk about everything; we are best friends and enjoy each other's company very much. But we were only able to do this after we learned how to deal with each other's baggage.

Renato Cardoso:

I noticed her jealousy, which upset me very much, but could not understand its root. I had no idea what was in her baggage. And so, whenever she demanded something of me, forced me to do something or accused me of anything, I would simply shut her out. This was when she began learning a little more about the baggage I was carrying.

I grew up watching my father deal with his marriage problems by shutting my mother out. I saw this all through my childhood. When my mother did something that he did not like, my father would "punish" her with the silent treatment for two, three, or five days. The longest time, believe it or not, was eight months! If there were a silent treatment competition, my father would be the record holder...

I hated it when they were not talking to each other. My mother would try to make peace and do things to please him, but he would not let go of what had happened—little things that were often nonsense. This led to a horrible atmosphere for us four children. I always told myself that I would never be like that when I got married.

And yet, when I got married I did exactly the same thing to Cristiane. In the end, experience is more powerful than theory. I knew what I was doing was wrong, but that's what I had learned to do and what I had seen all through my childhood and adolescence. That was the heavy weight in my baggage.

EXCESS BAGGAGE

The truth is, we are what we have learned to be. That was my reference point. We end up repeating our parents' mistakes because their behaviour (not their words) is our school. I did not want to act that way, but it seemed as if I was programmed to act like my father. Cristiane's apologies were not enough to change my behaviour.

In a relationship we have to unlearn the bad before we can learn the good. We have to identify our bad habits, what is not working, and eliminate them so that we can then develop new and better habits. This recognition is painful, but of utmost importance if we are going to change.

As you can see, early on in our marriage Cristiane and I had various problems because of the baggage we brought into the relationship. I was not a bad person, nor was she, but when we put our baggage together, the results were bad. This happens in all relationships. Every single person is lugging around baggage, their set of principles, values, experiences, culture, worldview, beliefs, habits, past trauma, family/school/ friends' influences, dreams, and much more.

When two people come together in marriage, most of their problems come from things in their baggage that cause conflict. Because of this, it is crucial that you get to know one another on a deep level and discover each other's roots, so that you understand why you behave the way you do. It is also crucial that you know and understand yourself, because this will help you develop ways of dealing with your own roots and, in turn, resolve any differences and conflict.

This is what happened with Cristiane and me. Years later, I became aware of our baggage and began to understand why we behaved the way we did. Her baggage was the expectation of a perfect family, which she came from, the image of a perfect father, the insecurities of never having a boyfriend (on the other hand, I had recently broken off an engagement), a childhood and adolescence with zero leisure time or social life. This explains why Cristiane expected so much of me, was jealous of women I had no interest in, demanded so much of my attention and couldn't wait to get out of the house and do something with me.

OPPOSITES ATTRACT, AND THEN CLASH

What's interesting is that her baggage clashed with mine, which is normal for most couples. Opposites attract, but once they're married, they clash and drive each other crazy.

My family was very different from hers. I had three brothers and one sister. We did not treat my poor sister, how can I put this, very gently. We were rude. My mother was constantly caring for my father and us kids, so rarely demanded anything for herself. She lived for her husband and children. My father... well, I've already told you about him. With this as my background, I found Cristiane to be a little boring, highly demanding, clingy and always complaining about nothing—bubble gum in my hair. The image of a strong woman who could handle anything was engraved in my mind because of my mother, and this did not help the perception I was getting from my wife, which explains my cold-shoulder towards and harsh treatment of Cristiane.

Another part of my baggage: I grew up around women. I had a sister, many female cousins, many aunts, female friends in the neighbourhood, at school, in church, and girlfriends here and there. I didn't see any difference between female and male friends. After marriage, this, and my cold-shoulder treatment of her, did not help the root of Cristiane's insecurities, which explains her jealousy.

At home, we were always a hardworking family. My father got up every day at five in the morning, even on Sunday. He put my older brother and me to work at the age of twelve. Hard work has always been in our blood. When I started working in the church, before I got married, this attitude increased, because now I was not simply working for money but to help others. Because I had married a pastor's daughter, I assumed she would understand the devotion I had to my job. But in reality, I drove Cristiane crazy. She did not understand me, and I did not understand her. For many years we tried to change each other, without success.

When and how did we finally overcome our differences? Only when we began to understand what was behind our behaviour and made adjustments to deal with the root of those conflicts.

I finally understood that her problem of jealousy and suspicion was my responsibility as well. I could not make her change, but I could reduce the triggers that fed her insecurities. I realised I could help boost her confidence in herself, and in me. I stopped debating and blaming her for her jealousy and gave up my friendships with other women, reducing my interaction with them to the bare minimum. I created a distance between me and all other women and used every opportunity to communicate to her that she was the only woman in my life. My goal became: Reassure your wife.

ATTENTION FROM THE OPPOSITE SEX

Many couples find this decision difficult. They are unwilling to give up on friendships that are putting a strain on their marriage. As a general rule, I learned that it is not wise for a married man to have close female friends, nor should a woman have close male friends. Having close friends of the opposite sex is playing with fire. It's common for people to resist the idea that this is wrong, because the truth is, we like the attention. We also believe that as long as we have no intention of betraying our spouse or getting involved with the other person, that nothing is wrong. We are far too confident in ourselves, and continue to forget that we are not in control of our, or the other person's, feelings.

So please understand: No friendship is more valuable than your marriage. Instead of holding on to close friends of the opposite sex, learn to become your partner's best friend.

Cristiane Cardoso:
I had learned this lesson in school from experience. At one point I got tired of my friendships with other girls because of all the gossip back and forth, so I started hanging out with guys instead of girls. On one hand, it was good because they respected me and didn't talk about everyone else's lives. On the other hand, some of them started looking at me in a different way, and I didn't even know it. When I realised that some of them had crushes on me, I had to distance myself and told myself I would never be friends with boys again...

When I got married and saw Renato with women friends, it drove me crazy! I was afraid he would develop feelings for them like my friends at school had developed for me. In the beginning, I would constantly complain, find fault, and use any weapon possible to distance him from those friendships. It was not easy to overcome those insecurities, but I did. But what helped me the most was to focus on what I was doing wrong, instead of focusing on him.

At times, a woman is right but the way she goes about solving her marriage problems is wrong, which puts even more stress on the relationship. When I began to change my attitude and focus more on myself, I was transformed into a more pleasant wife and Renato stopped tuning me out.

The great thing about this is that whenever we invest in ourselves, we begin to see what we are doing wrong. For example, I discovered that I had a calling, and that this calling was not about helping my husband timidly in the background but actively, right next to him. I began to overcome my own weaknesses, especially my shyness. My life no longer revolved around him. I took my place at his side and we had a common goal: To work for God.

Women do not always realise that whenever they get clingy, they push men away. Husbands will rarely put up with a direct attack from their wives. When Cristiane changed her behaviour towards me, she became more desirable. Soon I was more interested in her, felt closer to her and started asking her to go out with me.

This is when I was inspired to balance my time between work and marriage. I began to pay more attention to my wife because I knew she needed it. Overall, when we both understood the roots of our behaviour and did what was necessary to deal with them, the problems came to an end.

A HAPPY MARRIAGE TAKES WORK

Men are often workaholics, but we have to understand that marriage is also like a job, a business. If you do not work on your marriage, it will eventually go bankrupt.

Happy marriages don't just happen, they take work. When you see a happy couple who have been together for many years, understand that it is not due to luck. It is not because they "were made for each other" or because they are "a perfect match". If we take a closer look, we will notice that they are constantly working on their marriage. After 22 years of marriage, Cristiane and I continue to work on our relationship. Carelessness, being lazy or forgetting important things are enough to create minor problems. This is why we do not neglect this.

Unfortunately, many couples take each other for granted from their wedding day. They act as if they no longer need to make an effort to win each other over as soon as they are off on their honeymoon. OK, we're married! Job done.

Men, in particular, tend to do this. For us, the period from the first conversation up to the honeymoon is the most interesting for our competitive nature. It's exciting to know that she's willing to go out with us, that she's hooked and thinks we're awesome... It's like a game for men. (Women, I'm just being honest... this is our nature. You will get a better understanding of this later on in the book). And so, our wedding day is like a trophy presentation ceremony.

When a winner receives a trophy, he puts it on the shelf and it becomes part of his past. This is what many men do with their wives after marriage. We think the game is over, that the hard work of conquering her is finally at an end. We've even got a piece of paper to prove it!

Let me give you a friendly word of caution: The game has only just begun! If we stop working on our marriage, we lose the game...

TASK:

What are the main items in your and your partner's baggage—the things that have affected or may affect your relationship in the future? Take a few minutes to think about the major events that have marked your lives, or that formed your character, principles and values—what determine your behaviour. This task requires a trip into the past, careful meditation, and most probably a conversation with your partner to find out what his/her answers are. Write down what you are able to identify, but feel free to come back and add more things to this list, as you discover them.

/BulletproofMarriage

Post: I have started to go through our baggage.
#Bulletproofmarriage

@BulletproofMate

Tweet: I have started to go through our baggage.
#BulletproofMarriage
@BulletproofMate

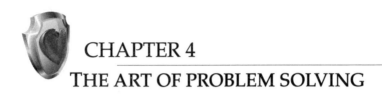

CHAPTER 4
THE ART OF PROBLEM SOLVING

Baggage, personality differences, tastes, expectations... all this and more set the stage for the problems that appear in a relationship. When they appear and you do not know how to handle these differences, they remain unresolved and the marriage will deteriorate. If nothing changes, within a few years divorce takes place. What is divorce if not an exit strategy for marital problems that the couple never managed to resolve?

Couples who once loved each other, end up separated or living together as strangers in the same house because they are unable to resolve the conflicts in their relationship. Instead, they insist on trying to change each other. They think: "If I can make my husband/wife more like me, then our problems will be solved." Then they criticise, accuse, point out each other's shortcomings, all the while defending and justifying their own actions. They run around in circles and never get anywhere. When one of them finally gets tired of the insanity, he or she decides to separate.

Being happily married is an art—the art of problem solving. There are at least seven billion problems in the world today—every human being has at least one, and most probably many more. Yet, we are all still here, and alive, in spite of our problems. We manage to solve some problems, and others we learn to live with until we hopefully find the solution. Problems are a part of life. Those who are the most skilled at problem solving are the most successful, those who are the least skilled, are often the least successful. It is no different in a marriage. If you want to bulletproof your marriage, you have to first decide to become an expert problem solver.

But note: Problem solving is not about changing people. Our focus must be to resolve the conflict between us and change the situation, not fight the other person. It is a mistake to think that we can change another person and tailor him/her to our liking. Not only will we be unable to do this, we will end up viewing the other person as the problem and reach the conclusion that we have to leave him/her and find someone else. If we do not learn to solve problems in our first marriage, we will go into our second marriage without this skill, encounter the same or other problems and have one more unsuccessful marriage. Is it a surprise that divorce rates for couples that get married for the second, third or fourth time continue to rise?

Our method is more effective: We want to help you to identify the real problems, find their roots, eliminate and prevent them from returning.

One fact that intrigued us the most was when we discovered that there is practically no difference between the divorce rates of Christians and non-religious people. A belief in God, the Author of marriage, does not seem to be enough to prevent people from getting divorced. This is interesting because if there is one group that should be skilled at keeping their marriages together, it should be those who believe in God. But why doesn't this happen? Because most of these people cannot, or do not know how to, apply their theoretical knowledge about love to their relationships. For example, it's one thing to know that God is love, and a completely different thing to know what to do when the person I love lies to me. A person's Christianity truly starts to be challenged when he or she enters into marriage.

MIRROR, MIRROR ON THE WALL

Marriage serves as a mirror. As you were getting ready this morning, you looked in the mirror at least five times (if you're a woman, more like 20...). Why do we look in the mirror whenever we get the chance? Because our eyes are unable to give us a clear picture of how we appear to those around us. If there were no mirrors, no cameras or camcorders, we would never know what our faces looked like, or some of our other body parts, or what we looked like from behind (though some of us would not find this a bad idea). But thanks to mirrors, we can look at true reflections of ourselves, and even see parts of our body that are hidden from our own eyes.

The same holds true in marriage. Our spouse is our mirror because he/she is a true reflection of who we are—the good and the bad. When you look in the mirror, you like certain aspects of your body and dislike others. When you put on a nice outfit, you look in the mirror and think to yourself: "I look good in this! These shoes match this belt perfectly..." But there are certain things that you do not like to look at. If you think your nose is crooked or too big, or that the gap between your teeth is too big or your hips too wide, you feel bad whenever you see them. I know someone who positions her head at a 45-degree angle towards the camera whenever a picture is taken because she thinks her head is too big... and like her, everyone deals with what the mirror shows them the best way they know how! But one thing is certain, it does no good to swear at or fight with your mirror. It's not its fault. It is simply showing you the truth.

When you place yourself in front of the marriage mirror, you begin to discover flaws that you were unaware of. After I got married, my bad temper was revealed to me. I had not noticed this problem before, because as a single man I had never lived as close to anyone, like a husband to his wife. When we were dating, we were close, but not as close as after we got married. The closer we are to the mirror, the clearer and sharper our image. This is what happens to all couples.

The problem is that up to the wedding day, all we hear from the other person is how wonderful we are. "You're so beautiful." "I love your honesty." "You make me feel so good, I forget about all of my problems." You only hear praise. So you start to think: "This person's going to make me really happy. I'm going to marry her." We expect to continue to hear only good things about ourselves after we get married. But the mirror does not lie. Once we're married, we are now closer to our mirror, and the other person begins to reveal our flaws to us... Rather than taking advantage of this opportunity and changing, we start to project our own flaws onto the other person and point out what they need to change: "He's so annoying!" "She's so spoiled, she cries about everything." "I don't want to act like that, but you provoke me." In other words, we blame the mirror.

It's only natural to get defensive when our flaws are being pointed out to us. Nobody likes that. But it's not smart. If you decided to ignore the mirror because it's always showing you things you dislike about yourself, you'd never improve. Instead of defending your actions and attitudes to your spouse, use their feedback positively. Take that information and improve.

As long as I saw Cristiane's pointing out my flaws as a source of irritation, I did not become a better husband, or a better person. But when I used my reason, I began to see that my wife was providing me with a personal challenge to improve, so I started using her as a mirror to deal with my flaws. You can do this too.

So please understand this from the very beginning:

You cannot change another person.

No one has the power to change another person. People only change when they decide to change. Whenever we get the sense that someone is trying to force us to change, our natural reaction is to resist. It's a way of protecting our own identity, our right to be who we are, even when it doesn't please others. I know this sounds crazy, but this is how humans behave.

"So is there hope for me?"—you might ask. "Are you saying my husband will never change?" "Is my wife always going to act like this?"

I'm not saying that he or she will never change. I am saying that it's not who is going to make them change. But there's good news: You can influence and inspire another person to change. That's why you are reading this book, so you can learn to do this.

Everything starts with a focus on yourself, instead of pointing the finger at your partner's mistakes. Just think: If you fix yourself, your marriage problems will be halved—even before your partner changes one bit.

When you change and stop demanding that your partner change, you will be taking the first step to inspiring change in him or her, without demanding anything. Let me repeat myself: Stop demanding your partner to change. Instead, look at yourself and admit your own mistakes. Open up your baggage and remove anything that's weighing you down. Don't worry about his or her baggage for now. First, focus on understanding yourself, so that later on you'll be able to understand your partner better.

You might have started reading this book because you're only interested in discovering techniques to change your husband or wife. But the truth is, you're going learn how to work on yourself. If you embark on this mission of becoming a better person, your marriage will improve, and this includes your spouse. But if your mission is to change your spouse, you should stop right now. We will not be able to help you. Nobody can.

CEASEFIRE!

When two countries are at war and want to look into ways of ending that war, the first step is declaring a ceasefire so that a peace agreement can be negotiated. They stop shooting at each other as a sign that they're serious about putting a stop to the hostilities.

If you attack your partner in any way, even sporadically, you should immediately stop. Here are some examples of what I mean: Sarcastic comments, accusations, verbal attacks, bringing up past mistakes and the like. But there are also passive forms of attack such as: The silent treatment, "forgetting" important information, indifference, staying out late, and so forth.

Think: How can you make your relationship bulletproof to external attacks, when you insist on making internal attacks? This is not wise. The external attacks that we're forced to go through are already plenty to deal with; we don't need to turn each other into enemies. Our enemies are the problems we're going through, not each other.

And so, if your relationship is at war, stop right away! Declare a ceasefire. From this point on, as you read this book, be civil to your partner and treat them with respect. This will give you a chance to breathe, gather your thoughts, and learn new ways to solve your marriage problems.

One more reason to declare a ceasefire: Avoid sabotaging your own efforts at bulletproofing your relationship. Think: If you continue to attack your partner as you read this book, your problems will only grow. There will come a time when you look at this book on your nightstand and say something like: "It's no use! I'm not going to read that stupid book anymore"—followed by the thought of shoving this book down your spouse's throat... Not good.

This is your new task to bulletproof your marriage: Ceasefire!

TASK:

Use the space below (or something else if you do not want to write in this book) to list the ways you normally attack your partner. Think of all the ways that you attack, from the least to the greatest.

_____

_____

_____

_____

I promise to stop treating my partner like this and to start treating him/her with respect, self-control and consideration.

/BulletproofMarriage

Post: I am starting the "ceasefire" today. #Bulletproofmarriage

@BulletproofMate

Tweet: I am starting the "ceasefire" today. #BulletproofMarriage @BulletproofMate

PART II

EMOTION VS. REASON

CHAPTER 5
MARRIAGE LIKE A SUCCESSFUL BUSINESS

Having a happy marriage is an art—the art of problem solving. Those with better problem-solving skills at problem solving will be more successful in their marriages. Those with poor problem-solving skills will have the most failed marriages. If you want to bulletproof your marriage, you have to begin by making the decision to become an expert problem-solver.

Problems are normally bypassed, ignored or postponed rather than resolved in a relationship. The cycle typically goes like this: A couple has a disagreement, they debate over the issue without much progress, tempers flare, one ends up hurting the other with words or with their inflexible attitude, both get tired of arguing without getting anywhere, they give up out of exhaustion and frustration, time goes by until the same disagreement comes back again.

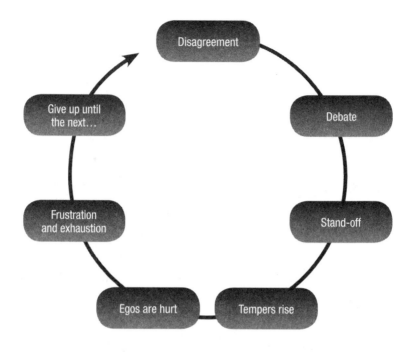

The seven-stage cycle of unresolved problems in a marriage

In this cycle, nothing gets resolved. The problem is postponed or temporarily fixed, but it always comes back. And when it does, it's almost always worse. Many couples think that time will solve their problems. "Let's give it some time," is an expression that many use when they don't want to deal with a problem. But marriage problems are not anything like wine. They never get better with time. When it comes to conflict in a relationship, putting it off will always make it worse. In this case, time is a couple's enemy.

One of the main reasons why people put off dealing with relationship problems is that they're normally extremely painful experiences. A lack of good communication skills, verbal attacks and anger cause couples to avoid the issue rather than face it. This is especially true for men. Many men run away from serious conversations with their wife because they're unable to hold a conversation on the same level. Women, on the other hand, become frustrated because it seems that they can never get their husband to understand them.

But it doesn't need to be this way. There is an effective way for men and women to solve their marriage problems and prevent them from coming back, without hurting anyone in the process. I call this method: Treating your marriage like a business.

THE OBJECTIVES OF A BUSINESS

Why would a person start his own business? What's the goal? There could be many. Earning more money would be an obvious goal. The independence of being your own boss would be another. Many feel the need to live up to their full potential and see a business as their means of accomplishing that. Others want to make a difference in the world they live in; they want to help others. One thing is certain: Every company has at least one goal. No company exists to exist. Everyone's searching for results and those results become the focus of everyone in that company—especially the owners. If there are no results, there is no reason to exist.

Marriage is also a business. No one gets married without a goal or wanting to see results. When a bride and groom think about marriage, they are actually thinking about goals, about making their dreams come true, like: Starting a family, having children, making your partner happy and being happy yourself, living with the person you love for the rest of your life and feeling loved, building a financial future together, having someone by your side in your struggle to make your dreams come true, enjoying great physical intimacy, finding a true friend in your partner, etc.

Cristiane:

Though Renato and I had the same goals when we got married, I had some expectations that did not match his. And it was exactly where we had differences, where we were not aligned, that we had problems. It's so important for couples to know each other's expectations for marriage. If we had sat down to talk about this before getting married, we would have known what to expect from each other.

At times, couples even talk about their goals but with the passing of time, expectations begin to outweigh the initial objectives. If they don't make adjustments and remind themselves of their goals, frustration will cause them to attack each other: "You always said this or that, but now you're trying to change things." Instead of dancing to the music, they each begin to dance to different music, and that's where things get complicated.

We recently organised The Love Walk through our TV programme The Love School. The event took place in more than 30 countries. About 40,000 people joined with one objective: Learning more about your partner through dialogue. This idea developed out of an experience we had a few years ago, when Renato invited me to a park to talk.

We had been married for more than fifteen years, but this was the first time we spoke our minds freely and expressed our desires and hopes in one conversation. He learned about my dreams, my worries, my problems, what I wanted and did not want, and vice versa. These were precious hours that greatly strengthened our union. After this conversation, I knew exactly what he expected of me. I knew what to do to support him and how to do it.

Many times we think we're at our partner's side, when in fact we're far away because of our ignorance of what we both really want from each other.

A marriage also has goals and must produce results, just like a business.

Why is it important for you to understand this parallel?

A company's goals guide its day-to-day activities. The decisions they make, who they hire, how they train their employees, the products they make and their advertising—everything is designed around the goals and results that the company wants to achieve.

When it comes to marriage, we found that most couples unfortunately do not have this same train of thought. They're caught up in their busy lives, they get lost in emotion and quickly lose sight of why they got married in the first place. Once their goals are forgotten, the decisions they make and the things they do no longer contribute to the happiness and success of the marriage.

When a husband gets involved with a lover, for example, he has clearly lost sight of his marriage goals. But this is taking place not only at the moment of his affair. It began at the very instant he decided to look at another woman and allow himself to be interested in her. That look caused him to wander off the path that would lead to the goals of his marriage. He lost focus and abandoned his company's goals. His persistence down this path will inevitably lead his marriage into bankruptcy.

If one spouse enters into the marriage with the thought that it might not last "till death do us part"—that person will end up doing things to sabotage the marriage, and cause it to end. If on the other hand, when a person sees himself by his partner's side till death, then he will do all he can to keep that relationship going. In other words, our focus on the goal determines our behaviour.

In the beginning of my marriage, whenever I had a misunderstanding with Cristiane, my goal was to win the argument. I wanted to prove that she was wrong and I was right. And because I'm a better debater than she is, I would almost always win. What a shortsighted goal. I would win the argument but lose my wife's intimacy and friendship. This is what many couples do: They would rather be right than happy.

When I learned that my marriage is like a business, I realised that even the smallest decisions and actions must be linked to our long-term goals. Today, whenever we argue, which is seldom, I always ask myself: What outcome do I want from this conversation? My goals come to mind, and I make sure the conversation goes in the direction that will achieve those goals.

HOW COMPANIES SOLVE PROBLEMS

Do you think Steve Jobs ran into problems when he started Apple? Of course he did. From Apple to the hotdog stand around the corner, every business starts with dreams and goals, but eventually encounters problems—and not just in the beginning. No matter how successful a company might be, it must address and resolve issues on a daily basis. The survival of any business depends on their problem solving. If problems are not resolved, the company will go bankrupt. In fact, if you are an employee, this is the real reason you were hired: To solve problems. (And you thought it was because they liked your resume!)

No matter how many employees a company has—only two, 2,000 or 20,000—successful businesses achieve their goals by solving their problems. But the interesting thing is, there is no loving relationship between employees. Often, it's the exact opposite. We hardly ever hear an employee say, "I love my boss!", nor do we hear of one co-worker writing love letters to another co-worker in accounting. Now, if they can succeed under these circumstances, they must be doing something right.

Question: *Why do couples with a relatively small amount of problems, who love each other dearly, often fail to meet the challenges of a relationship?*

Answer: Because they use the wrong tool to solve problem: emotion.

The secret behind successful businesses is that they avoid using emotion in problem solving and use reason instead. They understand that nothing can be solved with emotion. The workplace is a zone for intelligence and action, not a zone for emotion or this or that feeling. For this reason, they achieve their goals regardless of their employees' feelings, and regardless of whether one employee dislikes another. In these companies, you learn to separate work and interpersonal relationships, and never mix the two. They reason: "I don't like my boss, but he told me to do this, and he pays my salary. So I'll do what needs to be done." This means: They separate emotion from action, people from work, and focus on the desired outcome. They use reason, not emotion. Keep this phrase in mind:

Emotions are the wrong tool for solving problems.

Think back: Every time you made a decision based on emotion, you ran into trouble. Anyone who runs his business by emotion, fails. Have you ever heard the saying: "Never mix business and friendship"? This sums up the motto of many successful entrepreneurs. "I don't care who you are, whether or not I like you or you like me. What matters is that we have this problem, and we need to come up with a solution in order to achieve our goals. What can we do to solve this?"

This is what businesses focus on: _What are we going to do?_

What are we _going to do_ to increase sales? What are we _going to do_ to reduce spending? What are we _going to do_ to surpass our competitors?

Do. Do. Do. Not feel, feel, feel.

Feelings are not the tool to solve problems.

A DISCOVERY IN THE LABORATORY

We have a section in our programme The Love School called "The Laboratory". In this section, we tape couples arguing about the problems in their relationship. Cristiane and I watch the couple, identify the problems in their communication and behaviour, and then give them suggestions on how to improve. Before we turn on the cameras, we place the couple alone in the studio, they're seated and facing each other, and we ask them to start talking about anything they think needs to be resolved between them. Then we turn on the cameras. It's a real experience... As a result, we call it "The Laboratory".

A discovery we made while watching these couples was a pattern of intense emotion during the conversation and a lack of focus on solving the problem. Driven by feelings of frustration, anger, sorrow, contempt, defensiveness and misunderstanding, couples tend to spend most of their time going over their list of "Who's Worse". It goes something like this:

- *Wife:* You're so messy. You leave things scattered all over the place.
- *Husband:* The problem is you want things done right away. If I don't put my shoes away the minute I take them off, or put my plate in the sink, you immediately start yelling at me.
- *Wife:* You're so inconsiderate. Can't you see that I've just finished cleaning the entire house? The least you could do is not make a mess. You know I like things to be organised.
- *Husband:* You're not that organised. The other day I opened your desk drawer and it was a mess. So the desktop is organised but the drawers are a mess. That makes no sense!
- *Wife:* Okay, but if you'd help more around the house, you'd know how I feel!
- *Husband:* So I never help?

And this goes on and on and on. Ten, 20, 30 minutes later, and they're still going, jumping from one problem to the next. Note that their conversation never focuses on the problem or on what they should do to solve it. Emotion has one person trying to prove him or herself not that bad, or that the other person is not as perfect as they might think. In the end, it's the pot calling the kettle black.

The Who's Worse list

Pot: "You're black!"	Kettle: "No, you're black!"
Messy	Wants things right away
Disorganised	Yells
Inconsiderate	Is not that organised
Doesn't help around the house	Doesn't appreciate help he gives

By the time the conversation ends, the list is usually quite long, balanced, and both egos are wounded. Of course, nothing is ever resolved. No wonder many couples have given up talking to each other. Why talk? Why listen to the one you love go through his/her list of all your flaws? No thanks. I'd rather watch TV.

But, if they used reason instead of emotion, they would focus on the problem and how to solve it. At the end of the conversation, they would have reached a conclusion and would both know exactly what to do to avoid that problem next time. And... no one would feel hurt.

Now imagine, what would it be like if employees acted like the couple above when it came to solving their company's problems? The company president would call the VP of sales manager into his office and say:

President: John, our sales are dropping.

John: Well, why don't you get up from that comfortable chair of yours and come help us? Maybe sales would improve.

Of course, the conversation would never reach the emotional level of the couple above because it would end pretty fast, "John, you're fired. Please pick up your paperwork from HR." Because John doesn't want to be fired and his boss doesn't want to lose a good manager, they would instead focus on coming up with a strategy to improve sales. They would use intelligence and reason, not emotions or feelings—even though their emotions are very real and present.

Emotions are the wrong tool to solve problems—at work and also in marriage. How I feel about a problem does not matter. What matters is what I'm prepared to do about the problem. No one "feels" the solution to a problem. John does not walk up to his boss and say, "Leave it to me, I feel that sales are about to improve." If he did, he would also be sent to HR... Solutions are found by thought, reasoning, coming to a conclusion and acting upon that conclusion—never by following an emotion.

By using reason, not emotion, to solve problems, companies with tens, hundreds, even thousands of employees stay focused on one goal—and they don't even love each other. Surely, a couple who love each other and use their intelligence should be able to benefit from this tool, stay together and solve their problems.

TWO RULES OF BUSINESS SURVIVAL

Every business, every company, has to follow two basic rules to survive. If you break just one of these rules, you will lose your job or your business. What are these rules?

1. Identify, solve, prevent—Identify the problem (understand what it really is, and what causes it), solve it, and if possible, prevent it from reoccurring. This is the basic rule for a successful company. For example: Several customers have complained about long delays in product delivery. The company has to find out what is causing these delays, solve the problem, and implement standards and methods that will eliminate the chance for these delays to reoccur.

2. Don't take anything personally—In business, reason must be used. If you're emotional and take things personally, you will not be effective and will usually not last very long on your job. Your personal life, what you feel about what's going on at home or with your colleagues does not matter to the company. You have to learn to separate things. The focus of the company is its goals and what needs to be done to achieve those goals. Your boss expects you to be an adult, not a spoiled child who throws tantrums whenever something doesn't go according to plan.

Focusing on the problem and putting emotions to the side—this is how businesses survive and thrive. By using the same tools, your marriage can also overcome all challenges.

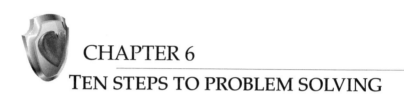

CHAPTER 6

TEN STEPS TO PROBLEM SOLVING

The two basic rules described in the previous chapter enable successful companies to thrive and advance on a daily basis by solving not only small, easy problems, but large, complex ones as well. We can divide the art of problem solving into ten distinct steps, which can also be easily adapted to the business of marriage. Any person who is successful at his job, whether boss or employee, already follows these ten steps, though most do not think of them in such a structured way. A focus on results and an emphasis on reason rather than emotion lead them to follow this natural process of problem solving.

An entrepreneurial mind is trained to follow this process without much thought, much like our legs go up and down stairs with hardly a visual clue from our eyes. But since emotions play a big role in our marriages, they tend to overshadow our mental abilities, making what is clear and logical at work not so clear and logical at home. Because of this, we will break down this process to help you understand how it can be applied to different situations in marriage.

We are going to compare two typical problems in business and marriage. This way you will understand how to apply the steps you use to solve problems at work, to your relationship.

Suppose you are the manager of the Human Resources department of a company named Gadgets Ltd. You are responsible for managing the company's employees. A problem is brought to your attention: There has been a high turnover in the company's receptionist position. Over the past three months, four receptionists were hired and then quit. The company is now looking for a fifth receptionist. The high cost of hiring and training, a drop in employee morale and the lack of consistency in the office are just a few of the negative effects. It is your responsibility to solve this problem. Your boss wants results.

Meanwhile, at Marriage Ltd., you are also facing a problem: He wants more intimacy and she thinks they enjoy more than enough already. This is affecting the couple's mood, causing him to be upset with her and causing her to feel pressured by him. Both want to settle this standoff.

Let's look at the ten steps to solving these problems:

1. Call a meeting and immediately talk about the problem

At the company:

The first thing you should do is call a meeting of the people involved and open communication to find out what is really happening. I want to emphasise the word "immediately". You cannot wait to deal with the issue because an overlooked problem will only grow. In the business world, quick responses are a big advantage over the competition. Therefore, you cannot waste time. Immediately hold a meeting with everyone who might have useful information about the situation—the hiring manager, supervisor, front desk manager, etc. You should do this regardless of how anyone is feeling about the issue. What has to be done must be done.

In the marriage:

Here is where most couples start making mistakes. When a problem surfaces, both tend to go their separate ways and brush aside any thoughts of resolving the conflict. They think that by postponing the discussion, they'll fix the problem. Men are generally more guilty of this, but it varies according to the problem. Women are usually the ones to point out a problem. They bring up the issue in the hope that their husbands will join them in searching for a solution. Men tend to be more simplistic, less concerned about details and have little patience when it comes to discussing things they do not consider a problem. In an effort to keep his anger under control and steer clear of an argument, he avoids talking about the problem, tries to delay the conversation or quickly finds a way around it. He comes up with excuses for why he cannot listen to his wife: "Not now, I'm tired, let's talk about it tomorrow." (Men sometimes do this in the hope that their wives will forget about it and leave them alone. So naïve...)

When a problem surfaces in marriage, you should take immediate action to solve it. Remember, problems are not like wine; they don't get better with time. Therefore, get together as quickly as possible to communicate and expose the problem. Eventually it will need to be solved, so sooner is better than later. If we wait till later, it might get bigger. So, act fast.

In this, or any other case, the couple should get together as soon as possible and expose the problem that they are facing in bed. Regardless of how they feel, feelings don't solve problems. What matters is that there is a conflict and your company cannot prosper when there are unresolved conflicts. Therefore, the best time to solve the problem, with few exceptions, is now.

2. Listen

At the company:

Step number two. After meeting with your team, you should listen to everyone involved (your hiring manager, supervisor, front desk manager, etc.) to find out why the receptionists are quitting. You want to listen to them because you're a professional, intelligent boss. One of the worst kinds of bosses is the know-it-all. Have you ever worked for someone like that? When he or she is made aware of a problem, they walk straight up to their employees with an order and a pre-fabricated solution: "From now on, you are going to do things like this." They don't care to listen to anyone, because, of course, they know everything and employees are just employees. But you cannot be like that. The best insights to a problem come from those who are directly involved with it. So, you want—you need—to listen to them carefully. Begin the meeting by talking less and listening more.

In the marriage:

Poor-skilled couples also tend to fail in this second step, and that's because of emotions. One of them initiates the conversation by pointing out the other's problem and the other immediately gets offended and defensive. This is where they go wrong. Instead of carefully listening to each other, they grow defensive until they get tired and give up on the conversation. While one partner is speaking, the other stops listening and uses that time to formulate his or her next answer or retaliation. They have stopped listening to each other.

There is a natural psychological explanation for why this happens. When we feel that we're being attacked, our fight or flight instinct is switched on. This is such a basic instinct that it can be seen in any animal. If you attack a dog, for example, his instinct of self-defence and survival will either cause him to attack back or run away. Humans use this same instinct for everything. So what does this mean? Whoever initiates a conversation has the power to determine their partner's reaction—positive or negative. A conversation that begins in an accusatory or critical tone will provoke a fight or flight reaction to the conversation. Ideally, the problem should be presented in a way that is not directed at any one person. For example, if a husband says,

"You're a cold person, you never want to do anything with me"—his wife will feel that she's being attacked and will be tempted to answer: "You're an animal, all you care about is sex." The war has just begun. Now, neither one will listen to the other; all they will do is attack and defend. But if he begins the conversation by saying, "Honey, is there something I can do to make our sex life more satisfying for you?"— her reaction will be different. Did you notice the difference? The way a conversation starts determines whether or not the listener is willing to participate.

When your spouse begins to expose a problem, resist the temptation to defend or justify yourself. Initially, just listen and gather information. Allow him to freely express himself. Do not assume that you already know what the problem is because the other person may have a different view of what it really is. So be smart: Listen.

3. Ask

At the company:

To identify and understand the root of a problem, you need to ask questions that will provide you this information. Do we know why each of the four receptionists quit? How were they recruited? Who hired them and what criteria were used in the hiring process? What was their salary? How does that match up with comparable positions in other companies? What's the job description for this position? How far along are we in recruiting the next secretary? In other words, you need to ask the necessary questions for a better understanding of the problem—and continue *listening* attentively to the answers. Notice how these questions are not accusatory, nor are they looking for someone to blame—they're simply aimed at gathering relevant information.

A technique developed by Japanese professionals states that if you define a problem and ask why it is happening at least five times, you're likely to discover the root of the problem. For example:

1. The house is cold. (problem) *Why is that?*
2. Because the heating system is broken. *And why is that?*
3. It hasn't received the proper maintenance. *Why not?*
4. Because I didn't want to pay for it. *Why not?*
5. Because I'm too stingy and don't like spending money unless I really have to. *(Root of the problem!)*

The immediate solution to the problem of the cold house is, of course, to fix the heating system. The permanent solution, however, is a change in that person's mindset about money. He needs to readjust his thoughts and understand the fundamental concept of "spend now and save later." If he does periodic maintenance on the heating system, he will spend some money now, but not as much as he would when the system breaks down due to a lack of maintenance.

Of course, he can decide to fix the heater now and not worry about the root problem. In that case, he needs to understand that the problem will be back in the future...

Asking "why" in an intelligent manner is a good way to discover the root of your problems and find a permanent solution.

In the marriage:

Asking your spouse questions when he or she brings up a problem that needs solving is a great way to not only understand the situation, but to show that you are listening and that you're interested in understanding the other person. It's the same thing you would do at your job—focus your questions on discovering the root of the problem. Are you satisfied with the intimacy in our marriage? What makes you feel that way? What do I do that you like/dislike? Does intimacy play an important role in our marriage? Why is that? How do I make you feel pressured? When do you find sex pleasurable? When is it not pleasurable? Is there a time of day/night that you prefer to spend time together? Which time of the day/night do you not like it? How often do you think we should be intimate—what is a healthy amount of intimacy? These questions will help you explore what is behind the problem, and will certainly shed light on other questions. Again, notice how the questions do not have an accusatory tone and are focused on discovering the cause of the problem without attacking anyone.

4. Focus on the facts

At the company:

In business, we work with facts, figures, data and evidence. Of course, intuition, experience, personality, principles and other more abstract inputs influence our decisions. However, our basic and most reliable decisions are those that are tangible, solid, real and indisputable. Because of this, your thoughts about the receptionist desk at Gadgets Ltd. are mainly based on verifiable facts, rather than assumption or opinion. If someone from accounting says, "I did not like the last receptionist"—this is not an important fact. The solid information that the HR manager hands you is much more important: "The last four receptionists claimed they were leaving because they found better paying jobs elsewhere." That is a fact—and a pattern. "Other departments routinely give the receptionist extra work and she ends up not being able to do her job, or the extra jobs, well"—says the reception manager. This is another fact.

In the marriage:

A typical scenario at Marriage Ltd.: The husband comes home from work and leaves his shoes, socks, and other things all around the house which his wife has taken special care to clean up. He rolls around on the living room floor with the dog and in five minutes he's messed up what she took hours to clean. Infuriated, his wife comes in and says, "Could you not be such a slob?" Even though she's being honest about the way she feels, she has not stated a fact. I've never come across a husband who works out an evil plan against his wife on his way home from work every day: "I hope the house is nice and clean because then I can make a big mess. Ha, ha, ha..." The fact is: He's not a complete slob. This is how it may seem, what she may feel, but the facts are: "He leaves his clothes all over the place when he gets home from work, and, he seems to value being home and relaxing after a hard day's work more than he does a neat and clean house." For now, whether he's right or wrong is not the issue, but rather the obvious facts that can be seen by anyone looking at this scenario, not only his wife.

We must be careful not to judge our spouses. In fact, if we really wanted to be a judge, the first thing we would have to learn is to focus only on the facts, the evidence. A good judge ignores his feelings and looks at the facts, nothing else. And yet, we frequently judge our spouses, and end up being bad judges because we always rule in our favour...

Focusing on the facts is another way to separate emotion and personal feelings from reason and the problem.

In the case of a couple who have a problem in the bedroom, the observable facts may include, for example: They were only intimate twice during the past month, even though the husband asked his wife about it ten different times, and each time she said "no". Maybe she feels pain during intercourse. Maybe the wall between their bedroom and their child's room provides little privacy. She may confess that sex is a low priority for her in the marriage and that she misses the friendship they had in the beginning. She might also add that she feels used by him when he pressures her to be intimate when she doesn't want to be.

Facts are facts. They are verifiable bits of information that can be observed by anyone. They are not opinion. This step leads to effective conversations and clears the way for a solution to be reached.

5. Explore ideas

At the company:

Notice how up till now, throughout the first four steps, you have only gathered information that enables you to understand and define the problem. Now you're ready to begin exploring possible solutions. In the corporate world this is known as brainstorming—an open group discussion aimed at generating ideas and ways of solving a given problem. Everyone is invited to contribute ideas, the more the merrier, until the best ideas are identified, and the best proposal is chosen.

Maybe your HR manager will suggest increasing the receptionist's salary so that it matches what other receptionists are getting paid. Someone else may come up with the idea of paying more than the going rate, while at the same time increasing the receptionist's responsibilities. Another might suggest that a job description be written and clearly explained to the next receptionist, and that other company departments be made aware of what she is, and is not, allowed to do. The receptionist manager might come up with the idea of offering a career plan as an incentive, as a way of showing that there are opportunities to grow in the company. All ideas should be expressed and given fair consideration.

In the marriage:

This democratic process of sharing suggestions and ideas is vital in a marriage. Many couples sin by wanting to impose their solution on their partner. A good leader knows how to involve his co-workers and employees in the search for solutions—not for political gain, but because he knows that two heads are better than one. In the same way, a couple should search for a solution that best solves their problem, rather than pushing their own agenda.

Looking at the problem that should now be defined after the first four steps, the couple should at this point ask themselves: *How can we solve this problem and prevent it from happening again?*

This stage is marked by its creativity and quantity of ideas. The couple should feel free to share ideas without fear of being criticised, condemned or ridiculed. After all, there's always more than one way to solve a problem.

The wife may suggest: Maybe you could try to spend more time with me like we used to do in the beginning. I feel closer to you when you do that. I know I have to be more understanding of your needs as well, and shouldn't push you away all the time. I am going to work at being more intimate with you because I know how important it is. Could you do something about our bedroom wall? That would help so much. I can't enjoy it when I suspect that our children are hearing things.

He could also give suggestions: Let's see a doctor about the pain you're feeling during intercourse. I admit that I say things I shouldn't when I get angry. I'll be more careful with my mouth. What can we do to balance out our needs so that no one feels imposed upon? I want to satisfy you. Can you let me know what feels good to you? I'm going to learn more about this and get the help we need.

It's possible that neither of them has the ideal solution. That's when one idea would be to get professional help, someone who could steer them to an answer.

6. Propose a solution

At the company:

From all the ideas that were suggested, you have to choose the most realistic and effective one for now. If a permanent, solution cannot be found, choose one that should at least last for a very long time. After all we've heard, let's say that you and your team arrive at the following proposal: Match the salary that other receptionists are paid, draw up a career plan for her within the company, and meet with the new receptionist once a week for the first three months to identify any possible signs of job dissatisfaction before they have a chance to grow. This proposal is chosen because it appears to deal with the main causes of the problem.

In a marriage:

Keep in mind that the best answer to any marriage problem is always the win-win solution. If one loses, both lose. So remember the company's goals, the team, not just the individuals. Similar to a company, propose the solution that addresses the cause of the problem.

The couple may then decide to seek outside help from a doctor with experience in intimacy issues. They decide to split the difference when it comes to their expectations, concentrate on pleasing each other and avoid making each other feel imposed upon. They will also insulate their bedroom wall.

7. Agree on a plan of action

At the company:

Now that you have a proposal, everyone needs to believe in it and its feasibility. It can't be implemented unless those in charge are in agreement. The question to be answered is: *Does everyone agree to go with this proposal to solve the problem?* Everyone involved needs to believe in and support the proposal.

In the marriage:

If having the support of everyone involved is important in the workplace, it is doubly important for marriage. But you do not need to agree on everything. Sometimes you will have to "agree to disagree". When this happens, start looking for some common ground. Take short steps. Many problems cannot be solved right away, and this process may have to be repeated many times. But do not allow disagreement in one area to hold you back from taking action in another area where you're already in agreement. This step must end with both of you saying: I believe we can solve the problem by doing this.

8. Define who will do what, and do it

At the company:

Who will do what, how and when? In successful companies, no one leaves a meeting without reaching a decision on these three points. Tasks must be defined and distributed to those responsible, so that everyone knows their role with respect to solving the problem. With the solution proposed in the previous step, as the HR Manager, you must seek the board's approval to increase the receptionist's salary. The person responsible for training and staff development will prepare a possible career path for the receptionist. The front desk manager will remain in contact with the new receptionist on a weekly basis to detect any problem. Deadlines are determined.

In the marriage:

She will look for a doctor and get treatment, and he will look for a good book that explains how he can be more sensitive to his wife's sexual needs. He will need to stop pressuring her, they will both be more careful about using harsh words, he will hire someone to install soundproofing to the bedroom wall, he will be patient with her and she will be more attentive to his needs. Of course, the "doing" is the most important part. Once again, you have to ignore your *feelings*, your will, and simply do what is right and necessary to solve this problem. In the business, the directors might not feel like paying the receptionist a higher salary, but if that will help avoid spending more on continually training new people, then it must be done.

9. See if it works

At the company and in the marriage:

Though a lot progress has already been made, the problem is still not solved. Up till now, all we've done is talk about the problem! And so, both at the company and in a marriage, after everyone has reached an agreement and has been given a decent amount of time to execute the plan of action, the results need to be analysed. Don't abandon the process during the eighth step, which is where most people are tempted to assume that they've solved the problem. Carefully track the proposed solution step by step and make sure it's working. At the company, a good result would be that the new receptionist becomes a long-term employee, and remains a receptionist or moves up in the company. In a marriage, the couple should start enjoying a significantly healthier sex life, should be less frustrated and notice a change in their mood, which will draw them closer to each other.

10. Yes? Continue. No? Repeat the process.

At the company and in the marriage:

By following these ten steps, you will likely solve the problem, if not completely, at least partially. If your problem is not completely solved, don't get discouraged. That is absolutely normal. More than one attempt may be necessary. The truth is, this process will never end because new problems pop up every single day in a business and at home, and we have no choice but to become experts in implementing these steps as we move forward.

I often hear people say, "I've tried everything. My husband is hopeless." "My wife is not going to change. I've done everything you can possibly imagine for her, but she hasn't changed." Wait a minute. Let's take a closer look at what you just said. *I've tried everything? I've done everything you can possibly imagine?* I don't think so. You may have tried three, five, ten different ways to solve the problem, but don't say that you've tried everything. There is always something different that you haven't yet tried. *"I've tried everything"* is an emotional phrase. Reason, on the other hand, refuses to accept the idea that there is no solution to a problem. So then, refuse to give up when the problem is still there after the first attempt to solve it. Repeat the ten steps, except this time you know what did not work the first time around. This is what we do at work all the time.

The 10 Steps

1. Meet and open communication immediately	
2. Listen	Uncovering
3. Ask questions	the probblem
4. Focus on the facts	
5. Explore ideas	
6. Propose a solution	Seeking solutions
7. Agree on a plan of action	
8. Define who will do what and do it	Executing
9. See if it's working	the agreement
10. Yes? Keep at it. No? Repeat the process.	

Reflect on these ten steps and you'll notice how there is a complete lack of emotion in them. They are a logical and rational process, not an emotional one. The beauty of this process lies in the fact that you already practise this at your job every day. (Nobody could run a business or hold on to a job without it.) You instinctively follow these ten steps already, though you might not think of them as ten distinct steps. Even so, you apply them several times a day, every day. You probably don't even need to *memorise* these ten steps, because you already know them by heart. You just need to transfer this knowledge to your marriage and apply it when solving problems.

THE TELEPHONE TEST

Whenever I suggest this idea of treating your marriage like a successful business, many have the knee-jerk reaction that it'll never work for them. They say, "I put up with people on my job because I don't have to sleep with them. I am not romantically involved, so it's easier." But if we take a deeper look, this is completely wrong.

Let's be honest: The real reason we control our emotions at work has nothing to do with whether or not we like the people we work with, it has to do with money. You don't swear at your boss or get into a shouting match with a fellow employee because it would cost you money. This is why every once in a while we see people explode at work—they no longer care about their jobs and are already planning to leave. So, the truth is that we control our emotions because we have the extra motivation of not wanting to lose money. Now, answer this question: What about finding the motivation to control our emotions because we don't want to lose our marriages?

This brings us to another benefit of viewing your marriage like a business: Seeing marriage as your biggest investment. Married couples tend to be more stable financially and in every other area of their lives, such as health, faith in God and family. It makes no sense to sacrifice your emotions to succeed at work, but not in marriage. What good is a successful career when you are not successful in love? What good are an abundance of material possessions when you have no family to share them with?

Let me describe a common scenario. A husband and wife are at home arguing about something, exchanging insults. Tempers flare. All of a sudden the phone rings. One of them checks who's calling, realises it's an important call and decides to answer. But before he does, he gives an order to his wife in an angry tone: HOLD ON, I HAVE TO ANSWER THIS PHONE CALL! He answers the call, and lo and behold, his voice has changed. In a polished, respectful tone he says: *Hello? Hi there, how's everything? Sure, go ahead, I have time to talk...* The person on the other end of the call would never imagine that two seconds ago this same person was screaming in rage! In other words, we do have the power to control our emotions in the middle of an argument with our spouses.

TASK:

Let's put the ten steps into practice. Identify a problem that has not been resolved. It may be better to avoid anything too serious, for now, until you gain more confidence and control over your emotions. Think of an issue that's not too sensitive, but needs to be resolved. Start by identifying the problem. Write the problem down in one or two sentences. Then, sit down and go over this problem with your spouse and make sure there are no distractions so you can resolve this matter.

/BulletproofMarriage

Post: I started using the 10 Steps to Problem Solving. #Bulletproofmarriage

@BulletproofMate

Tweet: I started using the 10 Steps to Problem Solving. #BulletproofMarriage @BulletproofMate

CHAPTER 7

INSTALLING A LIGHTNING ROD IN YOUR MARRIAGE

As the construction of tall buildings increased in popularity in the 18th century, the risk of them being struck by lightning also increased. People realised that the higher the building, the greater the risk of it being hit by lightning. After numerous fires and deaths, no one had a remedy or even understood why lightning was attracted to certain buildings.

The overly religious, who had no true knowledge of the subject, said that lightning bolts were "arrows of judgment from God" or that they were the work of demons. And yet, curiously, churches were the buildings struck most often by lightning because of their high steeples. The bell-ringer was usually the first victim... The problem was so serious that authorities began to warn people to look for shelter during storms "anywhere but inside or near a church". No one understood why, but according to the religious, the Almighty was targeting His own house or allowing satan to—not to mention that nobody went to church on a rainy day...

The actual reason for this had nothing to do with God or the devil. In 1752, Benjamin Franklin discovered that lightning carried electricity. Based on this finding, he invented the lightning rod—a metal rod that, when fixed to the top of a building and connected to the ground by a metal wire, would absorb the electric charge and redirect it into the ground, thereby freeing the building and its occupants from danger. God was thankful, and the devil laughed at the overly religious, who were left feeling rather embarrassed.

Emotion is a form of energy, like electricity. When tempers flare between a couple, the risk of "lightning" increases. If emotions are not controlled, they will result in outbursts that can lead to the destruction of a marriage. And like certain buildings were more likely to be struck by lightning, certain people have short fuses and are more difficult to get along with because they allow themselves to be led by emotion.

And yet, having a short fuse is not a good excuse; neither is blaming God or the devil for your negative emotions. We are all affected by emotions, and we are all given the intelligence to control them.

We are not encouraging you to repress your emotions. Nobody's a robot. Marriage is one of the greatest tests of our temperament, and it's unreasonable to think that we can simply keep bottling up negative feelings and not suffer some sort of negative effect. Sooner or later, you will explode.

Instead of repressing emotion, you should find a place to redirect it other than at your partner. Benjamin Franklin discovered that lightning was a normal occurrence, but that it was possible to redirect it to a place where it would cause no harm. In the same way, we need to install a lightning rod in our marriage so that we can discharge our emotions elsewhere. But how can that be done?

BEFORE THE LIGHTNING ROD

In the beginning of our marriage, we had no lightning rod. Sparks flew whenever tempers flared between Cristiane and me. Her lightning bolts were a demanding, insistent and jealous nature with harsh words added on. Mine were the cold shoulder and the infamous "silent treatment".

Whenever my emotions flared, I didn't know how to handle them. I'm a calm person and tend to remain quiet and accumulate negative feelings inside. And so I would not explode, I would implode. Because I didn't want to fight with Cristiane, I kept to myself. I would think about all I wanted to say to her, would imagine our conversation, but would keep everything to myself. (If I had expressed at least 10% of the conversations I had in my head, I would have solved the problems so much faster... Later, as I counselled other couples, I discovered that I was not crazy, I was not the only one who did this!) I was repressing my emotions. The lightning bolts were burning me up inside, and my anger was causing Cristiane to burn as well.

And so, I would stay angry with her for days and give her the silent treatment. At times, after accumulating a lot of negative emotions, I would explode and behave like a psychotic horse trapped in a burning stable. Can you picture that? Not a pretty sight.

We cannot be devoid of emotions. We are made of flesh and blood. But we must also remember and believe that we are intelligent beings, not animals that only have instincts to fall back on. If on one hand we are influenced by emotions, on the other our emotions can be influenced by our intelligence.

That is what I learned and began to put into practice in my marriage. These days, there are almost no situations where Cristiane and I provoke each other's temper. But the few times where friction or frustration does occur, my lightning rod is asking myself: *What's my goal in this situation? What end result do I want to achieve by solving this issue?*

So I remind myself: I don't want to be angry at her... I want to go to sleep tonight with my arms wrapped around her... Resolve the problem in a way that's good for both of us... I don't want to be upset and walk around the house giving her the silent treatment for the next two or three days etc.

When I focus on these goals, I end up using my emotions as the energy to solve the problem rationally. I use my mind to reassess my feelings and emotions, and then focus on the results I want to achieve. This process helps me control what I feel rather than letting my feelings control me.

Once I put my mind in control of my emotions, I began the process of resolving the problem with Cristiane. At this point, lightning bolts no longer exist. My reason automatically redirects them towards my goals, instead of Cristiane. Of course, this requires that I take a few minutes to collect my thoughts. If you have a similar problem, you will also have to learn to resist the impulse to engage in combat whenever your emotions want to use your mouth.

The message is: Find a way to vent your emotions at something other than your spouse. What I wrote above is what works for me, but you have to find what will work for you. For example, Cristiane has a completely different, but very effective, lightning rod.

Cristiane:
Whenever I get angry about something, I can't do what Renato does without praying first. So my lightning rod is prayer. I go into my room, or somewhere private, and unload my anger on God—not against Him, but as a way of venting my feelings. I have found that prayer is a channel through which I can take any frustration to God. After all, He is the Almighty, and can handle a woman's fury... unlike my husband. When I put this into practice, God made me see that every time I insisted on a particular thing and butted heads with Renato, I was not pleasing to Him. And so, when I pray, I unload my emotions on God, gain the strength to make the right decision and resist the temptation to turn that issue into a big deal. I give myself a cease-and-desist order and refuse to create a storm in a teacup because that storm will only attract lightning bolts of emotions... So, I decide to sacrifice my emotions.

By means of prayer, I stopped demanding things of my husband and started demanding answers from God; I stopped suspecting my husband of cheating and began to trust in God; I stopped using harsh words with my husband and started speaking openly with God. This has been my lightning rod ever since. It works, and I suggest that every couple use this method as well, especially women.

Women tend to be more emotional and less rational. This is why prayer is a great way to take back control of our emotions and begin acting more rationally. If you've never tried it, make a sincere effort.

I'm not encouraging religious prayers and rituals. What I am encouraging is no-nonsense conversations that we could never have with anyone else—no husband, father, mother or friend, because they wouldn't understand. But God, who made us and knows exactly what's going on inside, understands and gives us the strength to act wisely.

The best thing about this is that we're taking our issue straight to God. We're going straight to the Source. If we are unable to change or force our partners to understand, God can. There are things that only God can do, things that we are tempted to label as unsolvable.

I remember a particular instance where I was right and he was wrong, but it was no use because he refused to give in. The more I tried to explain, the more critical and upset he became. The "poor me, this is unfair" feeling came over me, but I made the decision to stop butting heads with him and go take a shower. In the shower, I had a serious conversation with God: "Lord, You know who's right and who's wrong in this situation. You know what really happened. So You have to be the One to clear this up because there's nothing else I can do. I don't want to fight with Renato. I don't want to do to him what he's doing to me. I want You to give me justice." When I stepped out of the shower, Renato still had that face of "I'm going to be upset with you for days". I didn't say one more word. I just went to sleep, trusting that God would sooner or later give me justice. The very first thing the next morning, Renato gave me a great big hug and asked me to forgive him.

CAUSING ANXIETY

When our emotions are not redirected at something that can wisely absorb them, we will either explode at our spouses or suppress them. But when emotions are suppressed, they cause anxiety, which is emotion at the extreme. Anxiety is a sense of constant worry, nervousness, restlessness and discomfort, caused by the uncertainty of what will happen next. Everyone feels it.

This is one reason why God created prayer, so that we could pour out our cares on Him. If we do, He promises to take care of us[2]. This care includes freeing us from emotional burdens and showing us how to deal with our particular situation.

Faith is not religious. Rather, it demands that you use reason. Once you learn to use your faith wisely, you can use your faith to solve your everyday problems.

You can be sure that there will be cloudy days, heavy rains and storms in your marriage. And when they come, they will bring emotional lightning bolts. This is inevitable. But you can install a lightning rod in your marriage to redirect that emotional energy into something other than your partner. To some, a lightning rod may be counting to ten, others might prefer prayer and still others may find that going for a walk works for them. In the end, you have to identify your own and determine whether or not it works for you.

And don't forget: Emotions are the wrong tool to solve problems.

---

[2] Peter 5:7

TASK:

What will you use as your lightning rod? Determine what it is and start putting it into practice right away.

/BulletproofMarriage

Post: I have installed a lightning rod in my marriage.
#Bulletproofmarriage

@BulletproofMate

Tweet: I have installed a lightning rod in my marriage.
#BulletproofMarriage
@BulletproofMate

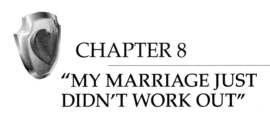

CHAPTER 8
"MY MARRIAGE JUST DIDN'T WORK OUT"

"My husband is great when he's not at home. He treats people well and everyone loves him. But when we're alone, he acts like the devil." A woman we counselled told us this. Her words echo those many husbands and wives who are frustrated by the two-faced behaviour of their spouse. This two-face syndrome is actually caused by a person's failure to correctly process their negative emotions.

When we fail to unload our emotions in a useful and positive way, they accumulate and we end up venting at our partner. We hold emotions in at work because we feel that strangers should not have to put up with our frustrations. Then we wrongly conclude that our spouses are obligated to listen and understand, no matter how we behave. This is why we show our worst side to our partners—demonstrating much less care than we do for strangers. We are well-mannered when it comes to strangers, and a pain in the neck at home.

Obviously, this attitude causes a lot of wear and tear on a relationship. Deep wounds are created, the couple grows distant and their love begins to cool.

Understand one thing: *The person you are at home is who you really are.*

People who suffer from the two-face syndrome tend to make their situation worse when they note the following: Their partner is always unhappy and complaining about their behaviour at home, but when they're among friends and colleagues, everyone looks up to and admires them (because they don't know their other side). The conclusion they reach is: "My partner is the problem. Everybody likes me, but he/she doesn't. I have to get out of this marriage."

And yet, the problem is clearly not their partner. If they gave their partner the same courtesy and respect that they give strangers, they would receive the same in return.

The person we are at home is who we really are. And so, even if this person divorces the partner who he thinks is the problem and gets married to someone else who seems to be wonderful and admires him greatly, this new person will eventually see his other side and have the same complaints as the first partner. If we are doing this, the truth is we are the one with the problem. Many can't see this and go through life marrying this and that person, in an attempt to find "the right one". But the problem is not that we haven't found the right person, but rather that *we are not behaving properly at home*. We behave in a rational way with outsiders, and in an emotional way when we're at home, projecting our negative emotions onto our partner.

This is why so many succeed at work and are complete failures when it comes to love.

I MARRIED THE WRONG PERSON

When a relationship starts to go wrong and people's partners don't change—refusing to put up with their emotional trash and with their every whim—the "obvious" conclusion is: "I married the wrong person."

"The marriage didn't go as planned" or "I married the wrong person" or "It turns out we're not soul mates" are expressions that exempt us from blame when a relationship fails. What happened to a sense of responsibility?

In the past, failed marriages were an embarrassment. When a couple had problems and complained to family or friends, the advice they were invariably given was: Go back, talk things over and fix it. The message was clear: Fight for your marriage. If the marriage fails, you fail.

Today, advice-givers routinely take sides and say, "How dare he do that to you? You deserve better. Kick him out!" "I wouldn't put up with her if I were you. Remember, there's lots of fish in the sea. If this wife doesn't work out, find another one!"

All these phrases carry the same message: If things don't work out, marriage is the problem, or the other person is to blame—he's not the "right" person. The new trend is to blame the other person and take no personal responsibility for the failure of a marriage. It's as if marriage were a person with a will of its own that can be held responsible for the success or failure of a relationship, or as if the other person could guarantee a happy marriage all by himself.

The truth is, both are at fault. Marriage is not a person. The two people involved in a marriage are responsible for its success or failure.

THE SOUL MATE MYTH

One idea that has helped people side-step responsibility for the success or failure of a marriage is the soul mate myth. The idea is that we all have a soul mate, someone who completes us and will make us perfectly happy. But where did this idea come from? Greek mythology.

The story goes like this: Humans originally had four arms, four legs and a head with two faces. Zeus, the "almighty" Greek god, feared mankind's power and split them in half, condemning them to a life spent searching for their other half, the half that would complete them.

Since then, most cultures have come up with a romantic concept that everyone has a soul mate, someone who shares a deep bond with you, who is naturally affectionate, caring, loving, and sexually and spiritually matched. The implication is that they are the two halves of one soul and they have to meet to be truly happy.

The line of reasoning for this myth goes on to imply that if the person I marry does not "complete" me, make me happy, understand me, and make me feel as good as when I'm eating chocolate, then he's not my soul mate. As a result, it would be useless to continue the relationship and try to make it work with the *wrong* person. The answer is to separate and continue searching for your soul mate—the *right* person.

This story may sound ridiculous and unbelievable, but I am convinced that this myth is deeply rooted in most people's minds. Performing arts are saturated with it, from Hollywood to reality TV, children's movies and romance novels. Who has never seen the typical movie scene where a bride enters the church on her wedding day, catches a glance of the groom at the altar, and is overcome by doubt because she knows he's not her "other half"? And as we watch the movie, we're all led to believe that her soul mate is among the crowd of guests (or at the airport and about to board an airplane, depending on the movie you saw) and we're on the edge of our seats, hoping she doesn't make the mistake of marrying the wrong person. Then suddenly, she turns around and runs away, leaving the poor guy at the altar, and is reunited with her "other half".

This has even infiltrated Christian circles, though there's no biblical precedent for it, where people pray to find their "other half"... Many remain single longer than they should because they're never sure whether this or that person is the one, and they haven't yet felt the "chemistry" with anyone. Some are even terrified by the idea of marriage. Doubt and fear are always present: "I am not sure if he/she's the right one."

The soul mate myth has gained popularity across a wide range of cultures and religions because the idea is romantic and attractive. The idea that only one person in the universe can complete you, and that God created you for that one single person, is beautiful. (But nobody stops to think: What if this person lives in Kazakhstan?)

It is not hard to understand what makes this idea so irresistible. It frees us from responsibility and blame when the marriage fails. "It turns out he wasn't my soul mate." That's it. It's not your fault. You just haven't found your other-half...

People don't want to work at it; they want things to come easy. It's human nature. Microwaves, instant coffee, diet pills... Happiness at the snap of a finger.

Based on this train of thought, people act on emotion not reason. Whenever they're faced with chronic problems in a relationship, they seriously consider throwing in the towel. "I tried, but it just didn't work out." "It's too hard, I don't think we're going to make it."

What do we do at work when we fail to resolve a problem? We try again. And if we fail a second time? We keep on trying different things until we find the answer because the company is counting on us and this is how we make a living. We don't give up. We don't blame others. We take responsibility for our work and search for an answer. We brush our feelings to the side and use intelligence, creativity and persistence in solving the problem. And if we're unable to come up with an answer, we make sure it doesn't affect the rest of the company. We do whatever it takes. We never give up. Never.

A persistent spirit, tackling a problem without fear and finding an answer at all cost, this is the key to success in work and business. Successful people do not run from problems—they face them. They know there's something to gain from every challenge; every problem presents an opportunity. They face difficulties with ease, are given greater responsibilities at work and are promoted.

When you earn a reputation for solving problems at work, everybody comes to you. You're the man/woman. Everyone knows that if they want something done, they need to give it to you. This gives you greater experience and respect and guarantees that you will grow as a person and in rank within the company.

On the other hand, when you don't take it upon yourself to solve problems at work, always make excuses and blame others, no one wants to deal with you. Nobody wants to hear excuses. You were not hired to make excuses, to point the finger at other people or to complain.

Cristiane challenged me to become a better person. I had to learn to solve problems that I had never faced before. I also had to own up to my mistakes and be humble enough to change. I persisted, but change did not come quickly. I had to give it several tries and continually resist the thought of quitting.

This is what we have to do in marriage. What you're learning in this book are things that work. They have the power to transform your relationship and you as a person. But don't expect immediate change, because it takes time for fruit to appear. This is a long-term investment—especially when you're fighting to save your marriage all by yourself, and your partner is set in his ways or sceptical about your changes. Don't expect your partner to believe you've changed when you started acting differently only yesterday. You have to win over their trust. Be consistent. The other person needs to see that your change is real and permanent. Accept this challenge—for your marriage and for yourself.

THE RIGHT PERSON VS. THE RIGHT ATTITUDE

The key to a happy marriage is not finding the right person; *it's doing the right things.*

If you do what is right for your relationship, your marriage will work. If you do what is wrong, everything else will go wrong.

When God created man and woman, He did not create them to be "soul mates". He first created man, then God decided to create a *helper*[3] for man, so that she could help him. He didn't say anything about

---

[3] Genesis 2:18

one completing the other, nor did He make one responsible for the other's happiness. He simply said *helper.* A couple should see themselves as helpers, and be committed to helping each other. When this partnership exists, the couple will be happy and the two will become one, *one flesh.*

> *Therefore a man shall leave his father and mother and be joined to his wife, and they shall become one flesh.*[4]

Notice that the two only become one flesh after they have been joined to each other. They were not "two halves" before they got married, predestined for each other. This miracle happens when both are united in the one purpose of making their marriage work, no matter what happens.

Obviously, if you're still single and considering marriage, look for the best possible person. (Please don't marry a psychopath and assume, "My love can change him.") The fact is, a happy marriage depends less on choosing the "right" person, and more on doing the right things.

Following certain laws of co-existence is what makes a relationship work. When God created man and woman, he established laws to govern their relationship. If you respect these laws, you'll be happy. If you don't, there's not a soul mate in the world who will want to put up with you.

Laws work like this: Obey them and they'll protect you. Disobey them and they'll punish you. If you jump off a ten-storey building, you're going to die. The law of gravity will make sure of that. If you go on a safari and get out of the car to take a photograph next to a lion, you'll end up becoming his lunch. The law of the jungle guarantees that. Whether or not you believe in these laws, you are bound by them.

---

[4] Genesis 2:24

God's relationship laws are not a mystery. Things like forgiveness, treating others the way you want to be treated, patience, serving, helping, listening, being unselfish, honesty, faithfulness, respect, assuming the best, removing the plank from our own eye before you complain about the speck in your neighbour's eye, caring, etc. are the basic necessities in a relationship. People know they need to do these things, but many don't. Instead, they break these laws and reap the consequences.

If you obey relationship laws, they'll protect you; if you disobey them, they'll punish you. It's as simple as that.

This is the only path. People may try to place blame on the institution of marriage, make divorces easier, invent new types of relationships, spend their lives searching for a soul mate—but the only way for a relationship to succeed is for a couple to respect the laws that govern it. This power is in your hands. It's your responsibility. Understanding these concepts was the turning point in my marriage—and it started with a phone call.

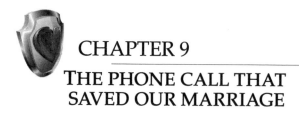

CHAPTER 9
THE PHONE CALL THAT SAVED OUR MARRIAGE

Cristiane and I never had a really troubled marriage. We did well most of the time and those who saw us would have sworn we were the perfect couple. We weren't constantly fighting, there never was any cheating and we had the same goals. And yet, from time to time, every four to six months or so, there would be a big falling-out over something. It was as if certain things just sat in the stomach of our relationship for months until they were coughed back up: Things that had never been properly digested or processed between us; roots of problems that we did not know existed and had never cut off.

Sometimes the disagreement was over her jealousy; other times it was because I didn't pay her enough attention. Now and then the argument was about work; oftentimes about how I felt disrespected by her, among other things. It was all leaves and branches and we could not see the roots of the problems.

When we had these big disagreements, we would spend hours speaking our minds in the bedroom. Tempers would flare. She would cry. If she raised her voice, I would raise mine even louder. It would reach a point at which we got tired, or at least I did, and the goal was no longer to solve the problem, but to escape that unpleasant situation. We would skirt the problem, but nothing was ever resolved. I would keep to myself for a few days, her eyes would be red from crying and everything would return to "normal", at least for another four to six months. This was how we spent the first twelve years of our marriage.

In my head, I was convinced: "She's the problem. I'm not doing anything wrong. She's stubborn and impossible to understand. If I stand my ground, she'll eventually have to give in and change" …and I made no secret of it. On several occasions, I told Cristiane: "You're the problem! I'm fine. I'm not doing anything wrong. You'd better get your thoughts together and figure this thing out because I don't have time for this." And she would answer with tears or by stating her point of view one more time.

I wasn't trying to be the bad guy. I was just really stuck in my ways. (It's a hard thing to be sincerely wrong.)

One awful day, which turned into a wonderful day, we had one of those arguments and the discussion lasted longer than usual. It was late at night and the end of our argument was nowhere in sight. Then Cristiane had an idea: "I'm going to call my dad." I thought that was a great idea. Right away, I grabbed the phone and handed it to her. "Go ahead, call him! You'll see that I'm right!"

From what I knew of her father, whom I respect very much, and the issue that we were arguing about, I was convinced that he would agree with me and say that she was wrong. Because he had never taken sides before, I saw him as a voice of reason. Though I was embarrassed about taking our problems to him, I saw her decision as a good idea.

I left the room and let her speak to her father. After about five minutes, she came out of the bedroom, calmly handed me the phone and said, "He wants to talk to you."

"Yes, sir," I said.

He went straight for the jugular in a tone that was loud and clear: "Renato, let me tell you something. This is YOUR problem. FIX IT!"

I was not expecting that. I thought he would empathise with me. I thought he would say that he'd spoken to her, that now she understood where I was coming from and I needed to be patient with her. But those words, "this is your problem... fix it," were like a red-hot branding iron searing my brain.

He didn't say anything else. I was at a loss for words, and after a few seconds, I said: "I promise you'll never receive another phone call like this because I'll fix it once and for all." I thanked him and hung up the phone.

"This is your problem. Fix it." His words rang in my mind. Suddenly, my eyes were open. "This is my problem. I have to fix it!" Everything became clear.

Up to that point, I'd always insisted with Cristiane: "You're the problem." My mind had decided that she was the problem and so I blamed her for not solving it. I automatically washed my hands of all blame. If this marriage fails, it won't be my fault, I thought.

Besides absolving myself of any responsibility, this mentality made the situation worse in two ways: (1) It gave Cristiane the power to do whatever she wanted about the situation (give up on our marriage, fight for it, continue the way it was), and (2) It gave her the impression that I didn't care about her and wasn't willing to do anything to change the situation.

If she had been another type of woman, she would have taken the power that I had unknowingly placed in her hands, along with the contempt that my attitude conveyed, and would have ended our marriage. Today I understand that if that had happened, I would have been to blame. Why?

Because I would not have fulfilled my role as leader and head of my marriage.

What that phone call taught me was that, as husband, any and every problem that crops up in my marriage is my problem too. I cannot assign some problems to me, and others to my wife. Every problem belongs to both of us. If she has a problem, I have a problem. If she's sick, I'm sick. If she has a complaint, I have to find out what it is, and quickly take action at the source of the problem—even if I think it's just her acting like "a woman". This concept changed my perspective on our marriage problems.

As a general rule, men have the tendency to throw a problem back at their wives and continue living their lives as if everything was just fine. A man's nature tends to make him avoid or run from a woman's complaints. This is why, whenever a man is confronted with a problem, he automatically points the finger back at his wife and tries to end the conversation. A typical male habit is to take his focus off his wife and place it on his job, sports, TV, video games, etc., as a means of escape. These men need to understand that avoiding or running away from a problem is not going to solve it. Again, I repeat: Problems are not like wine.

Men have to take charge of the situation and search for a solution to the problem along with their wife, as any good leader would do.

And that's what I did immediately after that phone call.

THE LIST

With her father's blessing, and my new perspective that the problem was mine and it was up to me to solve it, I went back into the room with Cristiane and was logical about things: "Let's make a list of everything that's wrong in our marriage. I want you to tell me everything that you're unhappy about, and I am going to write them down. Then it'll be my turn. When we have the list, we'll work together to get rid of each item on it." And we got started.

The final score was 6 to 11. She had six complaints about me and I had 11 about her. One more and I would have doubled the score. What's most interesting is that when we sat down to make this list, we made more progress in 30 minutes than we had in the first 12 years of our marriage. The effectiveness of reason is so amazing when it comes to problem solving, especially in marriage. That exercise was an act of reason, intelligence and zero emotion. It wasn't long before we started seeing positive results. Just the feeling of now shifting the focus off each other and on to ourselves was already a great start.

I'm not going to reveal what was on our list, but I can say that it boiled down to two categories:

1. Bad attitudes that we were no longer going to have, which saddened or hurt each other
2. Good things that we were going to start doing for each other, things that would please the other person and make them happy

It was as simple as that. This list helped us to stop looking at each other's flaws and to begin looking at ourselves, what we had to do to improve the relationship. Now that we had this list, our goals and objectives were clear. We both understood that if we worked together to eliminate each item on the list, each of us doing his or her part without pointing the finger at each other's flaws, we would no longer have those problems. The knowledge that we would no longer go through those painful episodes every four to six months was a powerful motivator. I was determined to do everything I had never done to solve our problems once and for all. After all, if the problems went unsolved, the heaviest portion of blame would fall on me because I was the leader and head of my marriage.

And yet, I knew I needed help from above. I couldn't rely solely on my own skills, because the list was long—17 items in total, not counting their little offspring... It was not going to be easy.

We finished our list around 2:30 in the morning and agreed to work on it. I put the list in my pocket, got in the car and drove to the church where I worked. I wasn't going to wait for the sun to come up; it was now or never.

I got to the church (yes, I had the keys), all the lights were off, and I headed straight for the altar. No one was there, just God and I. So I poured out my soul to Him. I admitted my mistakes, and asked Him for forgiveness, strength and direction for my life and marriage. I couldn't allow what happened to my parents' marriage to happen to mine. I would never accept that, and that's why I was there, asking God to place His hand over Cristiane and me. I held the list up to Him and asked for help. I felt spiritually cleansed. It was a very personal, real moment that I had with God. I left the church feeling light and strong. Though nothing yet had visibly changed, from that moment on everything began to change. I went back home, hugged Cristiane and we slept in each other's arms. The next day was a new day, the first day of our new marriage.

Things didn't change all at once, but we kept applying ourselves to make sure they would. It didn't take very long. Within a few weeks, we already noticed that our marriage had been reborn.

Up to this very day I still have my list, and as I was writing this chapter, I went back and took a look at it out of curiosity. It was a joy to see, once again, that all the goals we wrote down for each other have been achieved. Our vicious cycle of problems was broken; the roots were chopped off.

The power of understanding: "This is YOUR problem. Fix it."

Now that you understand this, I'm going to let Cristiane tell you about the conversation with her father in the next chapter. She's going to tell you about their conversation during, and after, the phone call—and how it changed her.

TASK:

The list worked for us, and I'm sure it can work for you as well. We often underestimate the power of writing things down, of putting something on paper. So now I want to encourage you to make your own list. Ask your partner what makes you a difficult person to live with. Write them down regardless of how you feel about them. If your partner agrees to do the same, share your feelings so that he/she can make their own list. Note: This is not an opportunity to attack your partner or to dredge up the past... Nor is it the time to get defensive. Your goal in this task is to compile a list of things you will begin working on to solve the problems in your relationship. Periodically, go back and take a look at this list, dealing with each item until you're finished.

Decision: From now on, I'm going to work on each item that my spouse and I have agreed to practise or get rid of. These problems are MINE. I will fix them.

/BulletproofMarriage

Post: I have written "the list" with my husband/wife. #Bulletproofmarriage

@BulletproofMate

Tweet: I have written "the list" with my husband/wife. #BulletproofMarriage @BulletproofMate

CHAPTER 10
MY PLANET'S SUN

Cristiane says:

When my father answered the phone, I tried to explain what was happening. But I was crying so much that I could not even speak properly. This frequently happens when we talk to relatives about our problems, when emotions cause us to fall apart. He quietly listened and after a few minutes, all he said was: "Give the phone to Renato, let me talk to him." You already know the rest of the story.

That phone call was the turning point in our marriage, but what really caused me to change was the continuation of that conversation with my father, which we had in person a few days later. The list Renato and I wrote down renewed our commitment to fight for a change and do whatever was necessary to please each other. But inside, I carried a deeper problem; one that I didn't even know existed. I only discovered this problem when my father came to visit and asked me how I had been doing after the phone call.

He never meddled in our marriage, but because of what had happened, it was natural for him to want to know. I replied that I was "trying" to change. I didn't go into details. That was all I said. To be honest, at that moment I was not sure whether or not things had changed. Often in the past, I had told myself that I would change but several months would pass and there I was demanding the same things from Renato all over again. Who could assure me that we would both fulfil our parts of that list?

Sensing uncertainty, my father got straight to the point. I'll never forget that day. We were in the back yard and he turned to me and said: "Men don't like women who beg for their attention. It makes you undesirable as a woman. Get busy helping others, doing something with your talents, work on your calling."

That was all he said and that was all I needed to hear. I realised that for all of my marriage, my world had revolved around Renato.

As a pastor's wife I went to church, helped however I could, did the "most" I could; but at the end of the day, my focus was always on Renato. All I wanted was his attention, to be appreciated, to feel like his partner and to be important to him—which was not too much to ask. But when these things mean everything to you, the issue is elevated to a whole other level. You end up doing everything with that person in mind, and if that person doesn't pay you the attention you expect, everything you've done seems to be for nothing.

Though I was not completely aware of this at the time, it was something I discovered about myself. Instead of taking my place at my husband's side for all those years, I had placed myself behind him. Obviously, he was not going to keep looking back to check up on what I was doing back there. The truth was, I had the wrong idea of what a wife should be for her husband.

I had heard many women say that we should be like the hanger on the back of a picture frame, and remain hidden behind them. While our husbands were out front, wives had to remain behind and provide the necessary sup-port. This is an old-fashioned idea without any real foundation. I am convinced that many women support the feminist cause for this and other reasons. If I had not woken up to reality, I would have done the same. There comes a time when you get tired of hanging around backstage, feeling less important than your partner and depending on him for your own sense of self-worth.

Because of my father's words, I finally embarked on an interesting, adven-turous and super-productive journey. I started learning more about myself.

INTRODUCING: CRISTIANE 2.0

I began to develop talents that were hidden or dormant. I invested in helping others and in myself. My self-esteem thanked me every time I took a step towards something new, different and productive. As I helped others and they found answers, they showed appreciation and eventually this helped me overcome my insecurities.

I stopped doing things to get Renato's attention. I was able to understand him better because we were now in the same boat, working toward the same goals. The only difference was that now I worked as a partner, not behind the scenes. I stopped focusing on him and focused on me, and how I could develop my talents and help others. I came out of my shell. It's amazing how a simple change of focus can transform everything. The problems that previously made me cry and complain, became so insignificant that they were no longer worth any of my attention.

One example was the issue of Renato rarely taking me out. Before, I would try to pretend that it didn't matter, but there always came a time when I couldn't pretend any longer and we would have another fight. After my change of focus, this was no longer a problem. I adapted to homebody tendencies. On our day off, I no longer expected to do anything; I would just find something else to do at home. I made videos on the computer, read books, rented movies, gave myself facials, etc. And guess what happened? I became a much more enjoyable wife.

It wasn't long before Renato noticed this change in me and found me more interesting. What was once rare became a normal part of our daily lives. Conversations were fun, we shared ideas, talked about our experiences, all without me having to force anything. I took my focus off Renato, stopped complaining about everything he was not doing for me, and focused on myself. This is when my eyes were opened and I was able to see what I was lacking.

For all those years, all Renato needed from me was a partnership. I honestly thought that I was being a partner to him until the point in my life when I discovered that partnership is not chasing after your partner, but walking by his side. This was why he didn't like sharing his day with me and didn't include me in his daily schedule. I wasn't in the same boat with him—I was riding in a dinghy behind his yacht playing catch-up. What I found interesting is that he had previously mentioned me getting more involved in what he was doing...

It's one thing to have your partner tell you that you have to change, and quite different to finally figure out how you have to change. A simple readjustment of focus transformed our marriage. And when I adapted to Renato's homebody ways, he also adapted to me. We began a healthy competition: Who could please each other the most!

I see this problem almost every day in the work I do with women. We seem to have the tendency to focus on others more than we do on ourselves. We can quickly go from one extreme to another. Some women seem to be on hold because of their love life, and others forget about their love life to pursue a career—as if we are unable to do both at the same time and be happy.

This is how many smart women end up as frustrated women. No matter how important a career might be, we need a partner to truly enjoy it. And yet, no matter how important our love life might be, we have to be independent so we don't become a pain in the neck to the person we love. If you depend on someone else to make you happy, you'll never be able to make him happy.

Your world cannot revolve around your partner. He has flaws, he can't always shine his light upon your planet and he can't supply everything you need. So it's unwise to put him in that position. You may even be doing everything right, which was what I thought, but you still won't be able to change your situation. Your eyes need to first focus on yourself, only then can there be real, tangible change in your relationship.

I've never forgotten a phrase I heard once in a church meeting: "As long as you keep looking at other people's lives around you, you'll always have problems."

HAVING YOUR OWN LIGHT

I remember speaking to a woman who found out after almost 20 years of marriage that her husband had never loved her. Her world collapsed. Everything kept falling apart until she finally woke up to faith. Many would have made a mess of their lives if they had found themselves in her place. But her story perfectly illustrates what I've just written about.

Imagine a beautiful, intelligent, gifted woman with character to boot—the kind of woman every man wants. She spent years of her marriage chasing after her husband, who didn't care about anything she did. Over time, she adapted to his strange ways, never imagining that they might break up in the future. She got married till death do us part and endured everything, and then some. Then, one day, out of nowhere, he revealed that he did not love her.

Instead of realising what had been going on since the beginning of her marriage, she was surprised, as if he had changed overnight. Why hadn't she noticed this before?

Women whose worlds revolve around their husbands have this disadvantage. They do not properly value themselves, and as a result, fail to establish boundaries. When you view someone else as more important than you, you cheapen and devalue yourself. That person holds all the power in the relationship; if he wants to hurt you, he can do it as many times as he wants because he knows that you'll never, ever leave. Your life revolves around him, and instead of investing in yourself, in your values and talents, you keep everything locked up inside.

Until she met her husband, that young woman had been full of life, dreams and plans for the future—an interesting girl who so captivated a boy's heart that he thought, "I want to spend the rest of my life with this woman." After they were married, she locked everything in a trunk and became a nag. She complained, tried to impose her will and found flaws in everything he did.

He didn't do it on purpose—nobody does. I, for one, did not realise what I was doing. On the other hand, I thought it was my job. It must be a part of our nature as mothers to always seek to make things right, to do something for our children and help them be the best in everything. Except, our husbands are not our children.

I am not saying that this woman's husband stopped loving her because of the way she acted, but it may have contributed a great deal. It's a man's nature to conquer… we'll talk more about that in the following chapters. As soon as his wife stops being something that has to be conquered, he will proceed to look for other challenges. In other words, she cannot let him feel like he's the centre of her attention.

A woman's value lies in her mystery, her discretion and the way she blossoms in certain situations. This is exactly what my father advised me to do: Men don't like easy women, even when they're their wives. When I began to use my time helping others and developing new talent in the process, Renato began to miss my constant attention. As a result, I became a new conquest for him. I began to have my own light.

There is no way for your marriage to blossom over the years when you as a woman do not blossom every day. With every achievement, every book I write, every project I create, I become more confident in myself and Renato finds me more interesting. I became that young woman Renato met in the beginning: Full of dreams, fun and a great companion for the rest of his life. This is what a partnership should be; this is what it means to be a team.

When Renato first heard that my world used to revolve around him, he glanced at me with a sad look on his face as if he'd just lost a very important position, and asked, "Can I at least be your moon?" Every husband wants your undivided attention, and in the end… though our world no longer revolves around them, that doesn't mean we should push them aside and just live our own lives. That's not what I did, and if you do that, you can forget about everything you've learned in this book because your marriage will be doomed.

What we mean is this: If you don't feel good about yourself, if you don't recognise your own value, you will always tend to make your partner your sun—your place of safety, and that is not an intelligent thing to do.

Even if your partner no longer wants to invest in your marriage and has already found another person, don't stop blossoming simply because he's no longer in your life. This woman, whose husband left her after nearly 20 years of marriage, is much more beautiful today, both inside and out. The break-up was actually good for her. The best thing for you to do is to improve while you're still together and possibly even win back your partner's heart.

CLINGY MEN

Women tend to make the man they love into their sun—but hate being the sun themselves. I know… I know… we love the attention, but when it gets too much, it's repulsive. No woman wants a clingy man.

Women want a man who exudes strength, independence and leadership. We might not always come across this way, especially when we're butting heads with his decisions or complaining that he always does what he wants. But on the other hand, if he starts granting our every wish… the relationship gets tiresome.

The other day, I was talking to a friend and found something she said about her current relationship very interesting.

—This guy is the "one", Cris. He has what the others didn't have. He's tough.

I was intrigued and wanted to know more…

—What do you mean?

—Well… the others always gave in to me, and things just got boring. But this guy's like this… I say, "Let's go this way so we can avoid traffic," and he says, "No, I have a route that I like."

I realised something I had never noticed before: We, as women, like to test our boundaries and see how far we can go. If a man gives us unlimited freedom, we lose all interest! It's not that we like to be controlled… but we don't like things to be real easy either. We can get to the point that we stop respecting our beloved partner. And so… men, don't feed us grapes while we're lying there with everything at our beck and call. The Cleopatra image is not okay.

The truth is that many men are unable to see their wives' flaws, and as a result, they never help them to improve as people. These men are also easily manipulated. Every time I made a mistake, I found Renato to be the partner I needed, someone who would point out my mistakes and help me get back in line. Women like that.

TASK:

How are you sucking the energy out of your partner and inconveniencing him? Take a few minutes to think about this. Write down what you're going to do to have more balance in those situations. What talents and healthy activities could you develop so that you're no longer excessively focused on your partner?

_____

_____

_____

_____

I promise to stop making my partner the centre of my universe.

/BulletproofMarriage

Post: My partner is no longer the centre of my universe.
#Bulletproofmarriage

@BulletproofMate

Tweet: My partner is no longer the centre of my universe.
#BulletproofMarriage
@BulletproofMate

PART III

TAKING MARRIAGE APART
AND PUTTING IT BACK TOGETHER

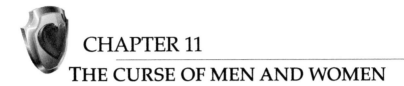

CHAPTER 11
THE CURSE OF MEN AND WOMEN

Like all other problems of humanity, the love-hate relationship between men and women began in the Garden of Eden. (I hope that Adam and Eve have a special, well-guarded place reserved for them in heaven, because I guarantee you: a lot of people are going to demand explanations from them...) Their disobedience opened the way for a curse that directly affected their relationship and those of all their descendants. First, let's understand what happened. I know that you already know the story, but maybe not from this point of view.

Before everything went down the drain in the Garden of Eden, Adam and Eve had a good life in every respect. The Creator gave them a position of privilege on earth, with the authority to do as they pleased:

...let them have dominion over the fish of the sea, over the birds of the air and over the cattle, over all the earth and over every creeping thing that creeps on the earth. So God created man in His own image; in the image of God He created him; male and female He created them. Then God blessed them, and God said to them, "Be fruitful and multiply; fill the earth and subdue it; have dominion over the fish of the sea, over the birds of the air, and over every living thing that moves on the earth." And God said, "See, I have given you every herb that yields seed which is on the face of all the

earth, and every tree whose fruit yields seed; to you it shall be for food. Also, to every beast of the earth, to every bird of the air, and to everything that creeps on the earth, in which there is life, I have given every green herb for food"; and it was so. Genesis 1.26-30

Man was given dominion over every animal and plant and over all the earth. This authority was shared with his wife: *"... and God said to them..."* This means that nature was meant to serve men and women. Nature was meant to serve them and meet all their needs.

And so, this beautiful couple lived in paradise and enjoyed power, harmony and the presence of God. They had no bills to pay and they did not point fingers at each other's flaws. Adam had the woman he had asked God for, and Eve had the man who... well, the only one around. In any case, they were a couple without problems.

But something had to go wrong, and to make matters worse, that day a snake was in the garden. Eve disobeyed God and led her husband to do the same. Time to settle the score.

First, God called out to Adam who was quick to blame Eve. However, the Lord did not buy this idea, thus stressing the point that a leader is responsible for everything that happens under his responsibility. Remember Chapter 9, "This is YOUR problem?" Adam had to learn this the hard way. As a result of his failure and disobedience, God declared:

Because you have heeded the voice of your wife and have eaten from the tree of which I commanded you, saying, "You shall not eat of it". Cursed is the ground for your sake, in toil you shall eat of it all the days of your life. Both thorns and thistles it shall bring forth for you and you shall eat the herb of the field. In the sweat of your face you shall eat bread till you return to the ground, for out of it you were taken; for dust you are and to dust you shall return. Genesis 3.17-19

In turn, Eve blamed the serpent. But it was not a good day for excuses:

To the woman He said: I will greatly multiply your sorrow and your conception; in pain you shall bring forth children; your desire shall be for your husband and he shall rule over you. (16)

It's interesting to note that the curse made man and woman subject to the elements from which they came—the element from which they were created: Man was subjected to the dust of the ground and woman was subjected to man, and this is where the man-woman curse[5] began. Let's understand the impact and consequences of this curse in a marriage.

A SLAVE TO HIS WORK

The curse that struck man was directly related to his work. Before the curse, there was harmony and full cooperation between man and the earth; but after the curse, the ground became man's enemy. Cooperation was no more. Instead there would now be difficult, hard labour—a struggle between nature and man. It was as if the earth would now reluctantly give its fruit to man, and frequently produce thorns instead of fruit.

This hardship would last a lifetime, until he would finally lose the battle and return to where he had come from: The dust of the ground. (Note that up to this point there was no death. Man had been created to live forever, but sin limited his time on earth. When God joined Adam

---

[5] Let me clarify: a careful analysis of the biblical text will reveal that God did not curse Adam and Eve. The text says that God cursed the serpent and the ground, not the human being. But even though man and woman were not directly cursed, they clearly suffered the consequences of these two curses, to which I refer henceforth in the singular: "The curse of men and women".

and Eve together, the plan had not been "till death do us part" but rather "for all eternity".)

Consider one of the aggravating factors: Man had been appointed provider of his family. This meant there was no way to escape the curse. He had to work—and he had to do it in the ground that had become his enemy. The pressure of supporting his family, being the hunter, supplying his family with everything they need, drives man to demand fruit for his labour. It's a matter of honour, pride, the admiration of your wife's parents and self-worth. The instinct of wanting to prove himself through his work and achievements is in the DNA of every man.

This is why a man's greatest frustration is professional failure. He may lose his marriage, be separated from his children and put up with a disability—he can endure all this as long as he feels useful and is a success at work. This doesn't mean he'll be happy, but his achievements at work will feed his ego more than anything else. This is his curse, his burden.

This curse makes him feel dissatisfied no matter how much he achieves. You hardly ever hear men say, "I've done all I dreamed of doing. I'm going to quit now." If he works day and night on his goal, applies all his energy and gets good results, he will typically say, "It could have been better." He never feels that he's made it. He's always demanding more of himself.

It's a common fact that many men develop depression when they retire, some get sick and even die shortly afterwards. It's as if their jobs were their life. Many refuse to retire and continue working for as long as their health allows.

Besides this dissatisfaction, men also compare themselves to more successful men and want to surpass them—or feel less of a man if they don't succeed. Men's competitive spirit is unlike anything else. No wonder the Guinness Book of World Records is filled mostly with men, especially when it comes to competitive activities. For you to have a better idea of what I'm talking about, there's a category in the book where men broke 16 different records, one by a team of 12 German gymnasts... What was the challenge? "The most somersaults into underpants in 90 seconds". This team has remained unbeaten since 2011, with 95... This is the type of thing you would not find 12 women to compete for.

So how does this affect a relationship?

You may have already guessed it. Isn't the amount of time a man spends at his work one of the classic complaints of wives? Isn't the "tendency to spend" (the money he earns by the sweat of his brow) one of the main complaints that men have about their wives? Now you know why.

In the beginning of a relationship, while they're dating, men see women as a conquest, a job to be completed. It's a competition—who will win the girl? Who will she choose as her boyfriend? This motivates him to work for her attention and heart. But when he finally conquers her and they get married, he turns his attention to the next challenge, which almost always has to do with his job. This is why he plunges into work and leaves his wife at home dying from a lack of attention. When she complains, he gives her a puzzled look and asks, "Don't you understand? I have to work, and besides, I'm doing all this for you." His answer is partly right. He works for his own sake more than he does for hers.

The curse of work makes men slaves to a sense of accomplishment, which they rarely achieve. During his search for this sense, he sacrifices family, wife, health and anything else. Ask a husband to talk to his wife about the family and their relationship and he'll be unable to come up with anything to talk about. Ask him to talk to a friend about work and he'll be unable to stop.

A wife can easily misinterpret this behaviour and assume her husband does not love her because he doesn't spend time with or talk to her; and because he seems happier at work and with his friends than with her and things that are related to her. But it would be a mistake for her to take this personally and assume that something is wrong with him, or with her. What should she do? How can she deal with this curse and help her husband at the same time? First of all, it's important for her to understand the curse that fell upon her.

HER HUSBAND'S ATTENTION

The curse that fell upon the woman is related to her need for the attention and approval of her husband. Putting aside the part about the pains of childbirth, which this book does not intend to solve (sorry, women!), the second part of the curse says: *Your desire shall be for your husband, and he shall rule over you.* This means you are always going to want something from your husband, and he will be your leader. Just like man became a slave to his work, subject to the dust of the ground, she became dependent on her husband's approval, dependent on him for the fulfilment of her desires and dreams.

Up to that moment, man and woman had never worried about "who's in charge". It was a harmonious union without the resistance of one or the impositions of the other. The two were one. But now, because of the woman's mistake, she was intentionally placed under the care and leadership of her husband, as if to remind her of the mistake she made by persuading him to sin.

I know this concept is taboo for most women, but the truth is, it could have been much worse. Just think: She's placed under the man who *loves her*? It would be much worse if she were placed under someone who *hated her*... Be that as it may, the concept of submission is a subject for a later chapter, which we hope will clarify the issue for you and remove the venom that's been injected into the word by feminist ideologies.

What this curse caused in women was the need to have their husband's full attention. She wants to be his princess, the chosen one, the most desired woman in the world, the one he risks his life for, and his reason for leaving everything and everyone if need be. And yet, she is rarely able to hold his attention for very long. Under the effects of his own curse, he is concentrating on his work, his next conquest, and still resents her for demanding his attention. He sees her as interfering with his goals. He gets upset because she doesn't "understand" that he has to work, and feels she doesn't properly appreciate him for his hard work and dedication.

When a woman yearns for her husband's attention, she unknowingly puts her self-worth on hold and does everything she can to attract his attention. She spends money on attractive, seductive clothing, make-up, hair, nails... but this is only the beginning. She cries, is dramatic, makes herself out to be a victim, gets jealous, is demanding, tries to emotionally blackmail her husband, stops taking care of her home, competes with her mother-in-law and even with the dog... These days, many unhappily married women are liable to have an affair simply to get the attention of their husbands.

This desperate yearning causes many women, considered intelligent and talented in their fields, to put up with men who treat them badly, in exchange for a little attention. This was the case of Rosanne, whom we recently helped in our counselling office.

She's an accountant. At the age of 34, she is the pride of her family because she's achieved so much in her career. She opened her own practice two years ago. She has more than 50 clients and employs a staff of five. She's a determined and capable woman. But while she abounds in determination and confidence for business, she lacks them in her love life.

Rosanne has been in an on-again-off-again relationship with Roger. He is 31 years old, has no achievements to speak of and is the incarnation of the perfect Casanova. He's handsome, tall and charming—a smooth talker who knows exactly what women want to hear.

Roger has no steady job or profession—unless slacker can be considered a profession. If it were up to him, there would be even a union by now. He's a talented storyteller who stars as both hero and victim in his stories. His mum pays his rent while he waits for the "perfect" job to come along. His dad pays for his car because "he can't get around if he doesn't have a car."

Rosanne gives him love, good food when he comes to visit, sex, and even buys clothes for him. Her boyfriend has to dress well.

In return, Roger has cheated on her at least three times, that she knows of. He tells her he's not "ready" for marriage. Every now and then he shows up at Rosanne's office, tells her one of his stories and convinces her to write him a cheque between a few hugs and kisses, swearing that this money is all he needs to start an exciting, new business venture.

Rosanne is like many other intelligent and talented women who fail to see how foolish they are when it comes to love.

Why do they subject themselves to this? It's the curse of women.

TWO FOR THE PRICE OF ONE

The two curses affecting men and women are in fact one curse: Insecurity.

At the core, men are unsure of themselves. Clearly, some show it more than others, but all men suffer from the same problem, even men who appear to be tough and resilient and to have strong personalities. This behaviour can actually be a mask for insecurity. Whether or not it is conscious, he shoulders the burden of the rejection he suffered in Eden, where he was the main offender.

A fear of failure, poverty and inadequacy drives him to work himself to death. The childhood voice of a demanding parent still echoes in his ear and makes him feel as if he will never measure up to his or her expectations, no matter how successful he might be.

The pride that holds him back from acknowledging his mistakes and learning from others worsens when he sees other men succeeding where he has failed. Anger, aggression, addictions, lies and other self-destructive behaviour are simply his way of dealing with the deep insecurities he feels. They are his attempts at covering his nakedness with fig leaves.

A woman's insecurity is easier to identify than a man's because she finds it easier to express her emotions. I know beautiful women who think they're ugly because one part of their body does not conform to the standards that women's magazines set. Others are jealous of anything their husband pays attention to. They are jealous of his job, football team, sister, car, the woman standing at the bus stop, colleague at work, ex-girlfriend—anything their husbands pay the least bit of attention to, and even what he doesn't—because of their insecurity.

Most women have low self-esteem. The same way many men use masculinity, strength and a strong temperament to mask their insecurity, many women rebel against their curse and declare themselves independent of men. "I don't need a man to be happy", "All men are the same—they can't be trusted", "No man will ever boss me around", and similar phrases form their mindset. However, deep down they remain unhappy.

In summary: They are both desperately insecure and in need of reassurances from one another. (Two thumbs up to Adam and Eve. Thanks a million!)

Now the most important question: how to get rid of this curse?

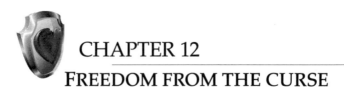

CHAPTER 12
FREEDOM FROM THE CURSE

I have good news and bad news. Let's start with the bad news. The first thing that men and women have to understand is that they are not going to change each other. Men will always be driven by their achievements at work and women will always be driven by a desire to to be the focus of man's attention. It's useless to fight against these facts. Those who resist move to the other extreme, which is no better. Men stop conquering and become weak, fragile and a disgrace to themselves and their family; women become bitter, hard, inaccessible to men and lonely. It's futile to rebel against the curse. You have to learn to deal with it—yours and your spouse's.

Now the good news: There are effective ways to deal with the curse. There are two aspects—one aspect, only you can deal with; the other, only God can do.

Let's take a look at what a husband can do and how his wife can help him.

THE STRATEGY FOR MEN

Throughout the Bible, God teaches men the key to being successful, which can be summarised in these words: "Work in partnership with Me". One of the clearest passages about this is found in Psalm 127.1-2:

Unless the Lord builds a house, its builders labour over it in vain. Unless the Lord watches over a city, the watchman stays alert in vain. In vain you

get up early and stay up late, working hard to have enough food, He gives
such things to His loved ones while they sleep.

There is the secret! God clearly says that men have to work in partnership with Him. Their success depends on their relationship with the Creator. Though they have to work, they cannot simply rely on their own skills, they have to also depend on God. When men work in partnership with Him, they don't worry about the result. After all, their Partner works even while they sleep! For this reason, there is no excessive self-criticism, insecurity or sadness because of what appears to be disappointing results. Men are no longer slaves of their work because they understand that their Partner is the one who brings growth. They have confidence, peace and the assurance that the future will be bright.

Women can help men by reminding them of the importance of this dependence. In addition to praying for success in their jobs, they should wisely encourage their husbands to have a relationship with God, because they will also benefit from this. The message that women must give, in their own words, is: "By yourself, you can only achieve what is possible. With God, you achieve the impossible."

Another concept that men have to take in and practise to counteract the effects of their curse, is balance. Men need to remember that there will always be work to do, and no matter how much we work, our work will never be done. If we work for 24 hours straight, the next day there will be still more work to be done. Men, especially married men, have to keep in mind that they have other, more important things in their lives, such as their wives. And so, they need to be balanced.

The Bible says that God created the Sabbath for "man"[6]. I believe He referred specifically to men, even more than women, because He knew that if He did not specify the Sabbath as a day of rest, that men would

---

[6] Mark 2:27

work seven days a week. God did not need to order men to work, but had to order them to rest...

Women understand the idea of the Sabbath only too well. If Cristiane would not remind me and plan something relaxing for us to do for at least a couple of hours a week, I would only stop working to eat and sleep. In the beginning of our marriage I resisted her attempts. I was unbalanced. I worked practically seven days a week. I would tell her that she had to get used to it, fit into my routine and conform. She wanted a little of my attention, I would give her practically none and then would get upset when she insisted that I spend time with her.

Men need to accept this help from women. They are a God-given resource to help them with their problem of balance. If your wife is complaining that you do not spend enough time with her or your children, that you are working too hard etc. She is probably right. Listen to her. Be balanced.

Another issue that worsens the curse is when men compare themselves to others, which they should avoid. Some competition is good. Having a mentor or role models who motivate you are positive things, but be careful not to constantly compare yourself to others. Comparing yourself to other men and measuring your success with theirs, is a recipe for frustration and insecurity.

We have to trust and develop the talents we possess, and not attempt to copy others. Learn more about yourself, develop your own identity, pinpoint your talents and work on them. Learn to celebrate the success of others, as well as yours. Learn to congratulate yourself for your accomplishments. Isn't that what God did when He created the world? The account of the Creation states that at the end of each day, God looked at His works and saw that *"it was good"*[7]. (And though He is God,

---

[7] Genesis 1:18

He set aside one day at the end of that week to rest.) When men put this into practice, it acts as a strong antidote for the curse.

Women can also play an important role to help their husbands deal with their curse. First, they should never, ever compare them to other men. They should never say, "You should be more like my father..." or "So-and-so's husband is really nice..." Ladies, this does not work. Do you really think those comments will motivate them to be better men? The truth is, they are like a dagger to their pride and self-esteem. This is worth repeating because it's so important: Never compare your husband (or son) to another man, not even in your dreams.[8]

Instead of comparing him to someone else, recognise and praise his qualities and achievements. Don't criticise and point out his failures in a negative manner. Be an encouraging voice by having confidence in his abilities. This is essential in good times, and especially important in bad times. Nothing brings a man down more than professional failure. Do you want to see a depressed man? Fire him from his job. But you don't have to go that far, just point out a mistake he made at work. After work, he'll go straight to the bar or plop down in front of the TV and feel like he's the worst creature in the world. Many men don't even tell their wives that they've been fired. They leave in the morning as if they were going to work as usual, when in fact they're searching for another job. In a situation like this, a woman can either raise her husband up or finish him off and bury him.

This reminds me of Cristina, the wife of the great Brazilian basketball player of international fame, Oscar Schmidt. During her interview for

---

[8] A civil war erupted and dragged on for years in Israel when women negatively compared King Saul to David. Right after David defeated Goliath and the Philistine army, he returned to Jerusalem victorious with King Saul and his army. Welcoming them with a great celebration, the women sang: "Saul killed thousands, but David killed tens of thousands!" (1 Samuel 18:7). King Saul, insecure as he was, couldn't take that unfavourable comparison and his reaction to it rushed his tragic demise.

The Love School, she told us that three months shy of getting a degree in psychology, she chose to drop out (after five years of college) and move to Italy with her husband where he had been hired to play. Cristina said that one motivation was the thought of her husband facing all the struggles and challenges of a new country while she was far away finishing college in Brazil. And so, she decided to prioritise her marriage. She left everything behind, went to Italy with him and never finished her degree. As she had anticipated, Oscar's team lost the first seven games he played. But with his wife by his side, he got back up and had a brilliant 13-year career in Italy, not to mention the international titles he won for Brazil. He was the highest scoring basketball player, an absolute success not only on the courts but also at home. He credits his wife for this: "Without her support, I would never have accomplished what I did," he said. The couple has been together for over 37 years.

Cristiane:

It's common for women to think that praising our spouses will cause their egos to go through the roof. Women are afraid that their husbands will become arrogant and self-sufficient. But this fear is a reflection of our own insecurity. We think that one compliment will make them think they're better than us. This is why many women admire their husbands, but almost never verbalise their admiration.

But with this new understanding that men are always chasing after achievement, recognition and self-approval, you can see how important it is for you to be at his side.

One thing I always saw in my mother was her appreciation and admiration for my father. She didn't pretend to be blind to his mistakes, but her praise was so much more frequent that my father's flaws seemed irrelevant and insignificant. This made my sister and I respect and admire him too, and was an example of how we should treat our future husbands. This is something Renato cannot hold against me...

When a woman becomes her husband's number one fan, she also wins, and in a big way. It's like a football game. When he scores and wins the game, he'll immediately run to her outstretched arms and celebrate. When he loses, he'll also run into her arms knowing that she will not be critical of him. She'll give him an encouraging word and the loving look in her eyes will melt away all his sadness. Now, who doesn't want that from their favourite player? Our female nature loves this masculine "dependency"!

This is where many women make the mistake, not because they want to, but because they think they need to be tough with their husbands. You tell him how handsome he is and he rolls his eyes as if the compliment is ridiculous. If you fall for that "tough" male exterior you might convince yourself that he doesn't need your compliments. But you would be wrong. He needs them a great deal. Men pretend to be tough, but deep down they want your compliments. Besides, who else will say these things to him except you and his mother? His co-workers?

When they don't react the way we would react, that doesn't mean they don't like it. Anyone can criticise him, but your criticism will be far more painful. The words of a man's wife will always hold more weight. Don't forget that.

When a woman supports her husband in victory and defeat, he'll never abandon her, unless he's a fool (in this case, he'll be doing her a favour).

THE STRATEGY FOR WOMEN

A woman's curse makes her dependent on a husband for her own sense of happiness and accomplishment. She will look for him for total fulfilment. But let's make one thing clear here: *No man can satisfy all the needs and expectations of a woman.* No man in the world could do this, not even if he were designed and created by a woman (her creation would be another woman, which she would also find unsatisfying).

The truth is, no man can satisfy all the needs of a woman, nor can a woman satisfy all the needs of a man. That would be utopia. Here's what I hear a lot: "I'm looking for someone who will complete me" or "My husband doesn't complete me". Stop right there. This person who "completes" you does not exist. Our life is made complete through a combination of things, not by one person. And no matter how complete a person's life may be, they will always have problems.

Women: Don't demand something from your husband that he's unable to give. Your husband is not responsible for making you happy, and you are not responsible for making him happy. Singles reading this book in preparation for marriage: If you consider yourself an unhappy person, please don't get married! Spare that other person from a life of misery. First you have to resolve your own problems, become a happy person, and then get married and share your happiness with someone else. Happiness in marriage is produced by a number of things, one of which is your husband. But there are things that he cannot do for you. For example, I cannot give my wife the things that God gives her. I'm not God. He gives Cristiane things I can't even imagine she needs, when she needs them, such as comfort, wisdom and peace. I cannot give her motherly advice. This is something she can only get from her mother. I cannot make her feel more useful and valued than what I already make her feel. But when she receives feedback from others she has helped through her work, her sense of self-worth increases. All these things begin to add up and she becomes a happy person—no longer depending solely on me to make her happy.

A woman's expectation to have all her needs fulfilled by a man is a curse in itself. And so, she should not run to this curse. Women need to discover those things that bring them fulfilment, like having a personal relationship with God, their job, a proper sense of self-worth. This will help you to stop smothering your husband, and he will start to find you more interesting and attractive.

Stop the excessive focus on your husband. Don't be like an octopus, clinging to him with all your tentacles. Don't suffocate him (one of the most common complaints I hear from husbands).

No value is placed on things that come easy. No one fights for what is easy. When a woman is too easy, she will get the opposite of what she's looking for: A man's disdain. But when she holds back and gives herself to him bit by bit, it keeps him interested in the chase. For example, don't insist that he take you out on a date. Drop hints of what you like and want, but don't beg for attention. A wise woman will make a man work to get her. A relationship has to involve motivation and the feeling of achievement for a man, just like his job. At times it's good for him to come looking for you.

Freedom from the curse means returning to the original state, before the fall in Eden: Man should go back to having dominion over the earth, instead of being its slave, and woman should go back to her position as man's helper and teammate.

When she becomes his helper in reaching his goals, she becomes extremely valuable to him, and this is when she'll get what she wants the most: His attention. Some wives prefer to compete with their husbands rather than join their teams. The main focus of their lives is something that does not help their husbands in anything. When a woman refuses to help and on top of it all gives her husband a hard time, she is shooting herself in the foot: She will become unattractive to him.

Cristiane:
Our problem is that we don't believe in ourselves. We always put ourselves down with words and thoughts. Many women think this is being humble, but it has nothing to do with it. This "humility" is annoying and bad for a relationship.

If you do not learn to appreciate yourself as a woman, all outward efforts are useless. You will be unable to appreciate anything else in life and will become a difficult person to live with. I've been there. I had everything, the wedding of my dreams, an exemplary family, health, and even natural beauty, but I did not value myself. So I would try to manipulate things. I would constantly point out problems in my marriage because Renato was not giving me the attention I wanted. I would accuse him of not loving me, and one day I even asked him if he wanted a divorce.

I could not see my own beauty. I would constantly change my looks, try different styles, and never thought I was pretty. I have photos from that time, and when I look at the clothes I'm wearing in the pictures, I ask myself what must have been going on in my mind. It's amazing how frivolous things like clothing and hairstyle can reveal insecurities. When I remember those times, I do not understand why I was so blind.

Only after I learned to truly appreciate, as I explained in Chapter 10, did I change. It was as if my eyes had been closed until then. I was able to see my potential—and what potential! If women knew their potential, they would not degrade themselves as much as they do nowadays...

"Who can find a virtuous wife? For her worth is far above rubies." Proverbs 31.10

You can be this virtuous woman, which I like to call a "V Woman". All you need to do is believe and demonstrate your worth by what you do and who you are.

How can a husband help his wife get rid of her curse?

He has to reassure her in every possible way. For example: Don't pay attention to other women, pay her compliments about her character and beauty, put her before everything and everyone, seek out and value her opinion, help her to invest in her talents and potential. In other words, pump up your wife's self-worth. Men cannot expect their wives to get rid of the curse on their own, without their help. Leaving your wife alone with her problems and struggles is not a wise thing to do. Sometimes, women seek out help from others because their husbands are not there for them (he may resent her for this, but it was really due to his negligence). Support and genuine recognition from her husband is much more valuable to her than anyone else's support. But if she sees him being extremely helpful to others, but not to her, her insecurities will increase.

Husbands need to understand that they are gaining by investing in their wives. There is an interesting verse in Proverbs[9] that says:

Where no oxen are, the trough is clean, but much increase comes by the strength of an ox.

Meaning: If you have no oxen, you won't have ox poo to clean up, but neither will you enjoy a harvest. If you want an abundant harvest, you have to be ready to clean up after the oxen... This is an insight into marriage. It takes work, at times it stinks, you have to clean up messes, but the end result is truly good. A happy marriage takes work. Men: This should be good news for us... We love to work, don't we?

COMPENSATING

Now that you understand the curse that plagues men and women, you can better understand why you and your spouse do the things you do. And now that you understand what you're each dealing with, you should help each other make the proper adjustments.

Those who learn to create this balance and work at helping one another, become mature and successful couples.

---

[9] Proverbs 14:4

TASK:

Meditate on what you have read in this and the previous chapter. How have the effects of these curses affected you and your spouse? Write down what they are and how you will deal with them from now on… instead of continuing what you have been doing.

/BulletproofMarriage

Post: Now I know how to deal with the curse. #Bulletproofmarriage

@BulletproofMate

Tweet: Now I know how to deal with the curse. #BulletproofMarriage @BulletproofMate

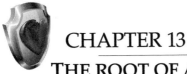

CHAPTER 13

THE ROOT OF ALL DIVORCES AND UNHAPPY MARRIAGES

If you were to ask a group of divorced people what led to the collapse of their marriages, you would get a number of different responses. Many would blame their spouse's infidelity, others would say they were incompatible; others would cite financial issues, yet others would blame their partner's lack of commitment. If we were to ask unhappy couples to list the reasons for their unhappiness, they would say things like "he doesn't pay attention to me", "I don't trust him anymore", "we fight all the time", "she's stubborn", and so on. Obviously, the reasons for an unhappy marriage are not always the same, nor are the reasons for divorce. But they all have one main root. The reasons couples give are simply consequences of a deeper problem, which is the root of all unhappy marriages and divorces. Psychologists and marriage therapists will not reveal this root to you. But the Author of marriage has already revealed it.

Identifying this root and cutting it out of your life is so effective that even if this is the only thing you learn from this book, you will have the power to transform your marriage.

POWERLESS TO STOP DIVORCE

In order to identify this deep root, I would like to point you to two passages from the Bible that may seem inconsistent at first glance. In the first, God allows divorce in the Law of Moses, in the first few books of the Old Testament[10]. Second, in the last book of the Old Testament[11] we discover that God hates divorce. Yes, that's the word He uses: hate. It is rare to see in the Bible that God hates something. When He uses this word, He means it. He really hates divorce. Why is that?

When a couple gets divorced, they might as well look God in the face, and say, "Look Lord, You made a mistake. This marriage thing doesn't work." Divorce is an insult to God, since it was He who initiated the covenant of marriage. It's a sharp deviation from what He originally had in mind when He joined man and woman.

But if this is God's view of divorce, why did He allow for it in the law He created? If He's the Almighty and truly hates divorce, why doesn't He stop it?

This was the question that religious leaders asked Jesus. Unlike you, they were not interested in knowing the answer. They simply wanted to trick Him into saying something that could be used against Him in court—literally. As always, they got more than they bargained for and Jesus' answer provided us a wonderful revelation about a controversial subject:

One day the Pharisees were badgering him: "Is it legal for a man to divorce his wife for any reason?" He answered, "Haven't you read in your Bible that the Creator originally made man and woman for each other, male and female? And because of this, a man leaves father and mother and is firmly bonded to his wife, becoming one flesh—no longer two bodies but one. Because God created this organic union of the two sexes, no one should desecrate his art by cutting them apart." Matthew 19.3-6 (MSG)

---

[10] Deuteronomy 24:1
[11] Malachi 2:16

With this reply, Jesus points out God's original plan and reveals the true meaning of marriage. In the mathematics of God: 1 + 1 = 1. In other words, when a man and woman are united in marriage, they become one person. The fusion of two individuals creates a whole new person. I am no longer the person I was when I was single, nor is Cristiane. Those who knew us when we were single can clearly see this today. We became different people (much better people) because of our marriage. There was a fusion of personalities. We often make an analogy to mashed potatoes, which nicely demonstrates this process. Two potatoes are just that: two potatoes. But when you mash them and add milk and butter, they become another element altogether: Mashed potatoes. Mashed potatoes are no longer milk, butter or just potatoes... There is no way to separate these three elements. That is exactly what Jesus meant by *"no longer two bodies but one"*.

The Hebrew word for "bonded" in the original text comes from the word for "glue", in the sense that two objects are joined together in a way that they can no longer be separated without causing damage to each other. Imagine tearing apart your own flesh. That's what happens in a divorce. It causes deep wounds that are difficult to heal, and great suffering in the lives of those involved. Marriage was designed to create a fusion, resulting in a third element—never to be torn apart.

Many want to get married, but also want to remain the same person. They resist the merging process and never become one flesh. They remain two distinct, unchangeable individuals within the relationship. This relationship is never going to work. I'm not suggesting that you give up your own personality and stop being you. The idea is to improve who you are by allowing your partner to influence you, by moulding yourself around him or her. It's like a child. He has characteristics of both parents—his dad's nose, mother's eyes, dad's hair and mother's skin tone, etc.—but he also has his own personality. The same goes for marriage. You end up a product of your union.

And so, when you get married, you have to have a "we" rather than a "me" mindset.

When you try to justify your mistakes to your partner and say: "This is the way I am. I was born like this, I grew up like this, I've always been like this, and I'm going to die like this... This is who I am"—you maintain a death grip on your individuality at the expense of your marriage. If the way you are is not good for your relationship, you have to find a way to change it—or there will be no way for your marriage except the highway!

"This is how I am", was my favourite sentence to end an argument with Cristiane. I would ask, "Why are you trying to change me? You knew I was like this when you met me." That was the voice of my individuality resisting the fusion into one flesh. Many listen to this voice right up to the moment they separate. Why the stubbornness? It is because of the root that Jesus reveals below.

A HEART OF STONE

Continuing from the previous passage:

*They shot back in rebuttal, "If that's so, why did Moses give instructions for divorce papers and divorce procedures?" Jesus said, "Moses provided for divorce as a **concession to your hardheartedness**, but it is not part of God's original plan. I'm holding you to the original plan.* Matthew 19.7-9 (MSG)

Here is the real root of every divorce and unhappy marriage: hardness of heart. Divorce was not a part of God's original plan. It was not an option when He created marriage. However, because of man's rock-hard heart, He had to tolerate—even allow—something He hates. Think about that for a minute. When you harden your heart, not even God can prevent divorce from happening to you! But aren't all things possible for Him? Why doesn't He prevent this thing that He hates? And worse,

He made it legal! Couldn't He have forbidden it from the beginning? God is not a tyrant. He respects our choices. He would never force His way into our hearts and make us change. But if God cannot help when you are hard-hearted, how can your spouse? You're the only one who can do something about this and avoid the disaster.

But first you need to understand what hard-heartedness is. What causes hardness of heart? Could you be hard-hearted and not see it?

A great many things can cause hardness of heart. When we speak about the heart, we're referring to the centre of emotions and feelings inside of us. Any negative feeling that has not been properly processed and eliminated ends up turning our hearts into stone. One in particular, is pride.

Pride turns hearts into concrete. Proud people are blind to their mistakes. In general, they think they are unusually humble and yet others are always in the wrong. They are always the misunderstood victims; they don't like to admit their mistakes and would rather have a tooth pulled without anaesthesia than to apologise. Because they are always right, proud people wait for others to give in and back off. They can't see how important it is for someone who's been hurt to have their offender acknowledge their mistake and apologise. Many problems would be quickly solved if the proud person would simply say: "I'm sorry. I messed up. I won't do that again." Instead, the proud choose to further harden their hearts.

I remember an elderly couple whose marriage had been arranged when the girl was 14. The family was worried about her strong personality and thought that marriage would be a good way to "discipline" her. Poor guy! They had their first fight on their honeymoon (did you expect it would take longer than that?). He said something silly about his childhood sweetheart being the only girl he had ever loved, and how he used to bring her fruits as gifts when he was ten years old. This "revelation" hurt her and stayed bottled up inside for decades: "He doesn't love me. He'll never love me." He never apologised because he felt she was being silly. She did everything in her power to make his life a living hell because she had felt attacked.

What did they gain by doing this? A ruined marriage… a shattered family… years of unnecessary suffering. He looked elsewhere for the attention he wasn't getting at home and she put up with her husband's many affairs, piling one hurtful feeling on top of another. Though they loved each other, neither one gave in. Life passed them by and only towards the very end did they realise that they'd missed out on years of happiness.

How many opportunities proud people miss out on! Little do they know that life could be easier and happier if they would just ease up on their spouse. They could learn new things, discover new ways of looking at life… Or why else would God decide to join two so very different beings together—man and woman?

If you think about it, it might seem like marriage is God's way of playing a cruel joke on us. It's almost like the Father, Son and Holy Spirit got up to mischief one day, rubbed Their hands together and said: "Here's an idea! Let's create man. He could be like this and that… Okay! Now let's create woman… she could be… the exact opposite! OK. Let's see what happens! They'll have to live in the same house. Oh, and let's make a rule: they can't ever separate! This will be fun!…" But of course, that's not what happened. There is an actual purpose for marriage, and a very good one.

God put two completely different people together so that one would challenge the other to be a better person. The idea was not to torture the people He created. He made us different so that we would complement each other. But you can only live with your spouse and improve as a person when your heart is open and flexible. You need a good dose of humility to kill this bad root and enjoy the best of what marriage is all about.

Let us take another look at the elderly couple's example. The problem started when the husband made a dumb comment. If he had swallowed his pride and made a heartfelt apology to his wife, he would have avoided 50 years of living hell. On the other hand, if she had refused to take his dumb comment so seriously and treated her husband with respect and affection, he would have had no choice but to make her happy.

Selfishness, pride's cousin, also has the power to harden a heart. A selfish person is guided by the following maxims: *What matters is what I want, what is good for me, and my wishes first.* A selfish person doesn't care about another person's point of view. He hears but doesn't listen, because his ego speaks louder than anyone else and drowns out his partner's voice.

In the beginning of my marriage, I wasn't concerned about the needs of my wife. As long as I was happy at work, everything would be just fine. I thought, as long as she had everything she needs at home, she has no reason to complain. If you believe your spouse has nothing to complain about because you buy her this or give her that… understand one thing: What's the point in giving your spouse a lot of what she already has, and none of what she really needs?

I met a young man who thought his wife was happy. Then one day he got a shock when his wife announced that she was leaving him. Conspiracy theories began to pop up in his mind. Who had talked his perfect and submissive wife into leaving him after six years? Was it her brother? One of her friends? The pastor? The son from her first marriage whom he'd never got along with? It was so unfair, he thought. He had been such a great husband, always given her everything, stood by her side, was consistently nice to her, and now she was going to leave him without any explanations.

What he did not realise was that she had felt left out for most of their years of marriage. She explained that everything her husband did and said revolved around him. He was not interested in what she liked or wanted. They did not communicate and he felt he was much smarter than her—at least that's the impression he gave—and he would force her go accompany him on cultural tours, something she hated. She was wrong for never letting him know how she felt about those trips. But if he had looked beyond his own navel, he would have noticed that there was an unhappy, neglected woman at his side.

Make a note of this: You gave up the right to think only about yourself the day you signed the marriage papers.

I WILL NOT CHANGE

Hardness of heart is stubbornness, insisting on something that does not work. It causes husbands to declare that they will not change, even when they see their marriage going down the drain. It causes wives to be set in their ways, refusing to listen to what their husbands are asking of them. If the way you act is not good for your marriage, and you don't want to change, know that you are destined to die alone.

We frequently harden our hearts in self-defence. After being hurt so much, perhaps by hurts, infidelity, lies, harsh words, or other painful experience at the hands of our partners, it's natural for our hearts to become hardened. We become distant and emotionally disconnected as a way of preventing that person from hurting us again. The problem is that building walls to protect our hearts is not wise—unless you want to be trapped inside, alone, with all those bad feelings, like a prisoner in a haunted house. Those who build walls end up building a prison for themselves.

Think about it: If your spouse is truly determined to hurt you and you see no more reason to fight for the marriage, then leave him once and for all. But if you're still willing to try because you believe there's hope, then you have to tear down the walls and soften your heart. If you live with your partner and insist on keeping your walls up, you must really like to suffer. Remember: If your heart remains hardened, not even God can help you.

Examine your heart and see if perhaps it's been hardened by any of these things:

- Pride
- Selfishness
- Being set in your ways
- Defensiveness
- Unbending in your point of view
- Being unforgiving
- A tendency to resist and/or deny physical intimacy
- Inflexibility (unwillingness to change)
- An "I'm never wrong" attitude
- A taker, not a giver
- A tendency to dwell on the past
- A tendency to build walls to keep your partner out
- Insincerity (you hide your feelings)
- Finger-pointing (your partner's flaws)
- An inability to apologise
- Uncaring (about your partner's feelings)
- An unwillingness to listen
- Constantly trying to change your partner
- You've made up your mind about an issue and will not change it (defending your position as the only valid one, of course)
- A habit of emotional blackmail
- A controlling nature
- A "this is the way I am" attitude to excuse any inappropriate behaviour
- An inability to admit you need help
- A tendency to use cutting words

- An emotionally cold and distant nature
- An inability to open up and share your feelings with your partner

Take a look at yourself with these points in mind. Make an honest examination of your heart. Are there any stones that need to be broken? What would your spouse say about you if he or she went through this list? As long as your heart is hardened, you will never be happy in your love life.

Cristiane:

To further complicate this situation, there are two types of hard-heartedness: Those who are clearly hard of heart, whose attitude is visible to all, and those who see themselves as victims. Both are hardened and very accusatory of their partners.

This is what happened with Renato and me. For the first 12 years of our marriage, I blamed him for not being the husband I needed him to be. His way of attempting to solve our problems was terrible. He would ignore me for days, and in the end I was always the one to apologise. I would apologise so that our marriage could move forward, but I wasn't wholehearted about it. I continued to believe that he was the problem, and was always praying for him (feeling righteous in my own eyes). I felt like an undervalued wife, because I gave so much of myself and hardly got anything back. I even wrote a sad, depressing song for the soundtrack of our "love" story. Then came the phone call from Chapter 9. After that I changed, began focusing on what I could do, and found out that I also had been hard-hearted for all those years. But mine was the victim type.

Yes, Renato should have given me the proper attention. No, he should not have punished me by not speaking to me for days after I did something he didn't like. But what good is it to know that your spouse is failing in his responsibilities, when you are doing the same?

At first, this revelation scared me. I had always considered myself to be a great wife to Renato. I always gave him my best. How could I have been harsh and mean to him? This is where many get stuck in a vicious cycle of frustration. Love is giving. But when you get to the point that you stop giving, and each of you is waiting for the other person to start giving again… it's over. You will continue going round and round, a real 360° "change"! You will change for a couple of months, but then you go right back to where you started from.

My hard-heartedness insisted that Renato change. I constantly demanded things of him. Whenever I did something for him, I'd sit back and watch for what he was going to do for me. And if I didn't get anything in return, I would go right back to my demanding ways. And you know, there are various ways of being demanding. You can complain, make an ugly face, make a few indirect comments, use emotional blackmail, make comparisons, and so on, and so on. All these attitudes come from the victim type of hard-heartedness.

I believe this is the worst type, because these people cannot see what they're doing. We think we're right. We raise the "how long do I have to be the only one giving?" flag—but what are we accomplishing when we give with our right hand and demand with our left?

I had this kind of hard-heartedness, and that's why our problems lasted as long as they did. I know that for a fact. In fact, as soon as I softened my heart, Renato changed, and my marriage was transformed. I had been blocking my prayers and all our attempts to change.

My change was simple. I believe that change is easier for the victim than it is for the defensive person. I simply stopped imposing. I sacrificed what I felt he should do, stopped pointing the finger and being demanding. Simple! That was it. And what did I get in return? We're here writing a book on the subject. Obviously, it was worth it!

Those who give in first will have the privilege of telling others what I am about to tell you right now: I changed first, clearing the way for my husband to change as well. Not everyone is able to do this.

GETTING RID OF THE STONES

If you acknowledge that there are stones and walls in your heart and you want to change, the first step is to get help from the One who hates divorce. Remember Him? Since God hates divorce, we can safely conclude that He also hates the hard-heartedness responsible for so many broken marriages. Clearly, God wants to help you overcome this. Here's what He says:

I will give you a new heart and put a new spirit within you; I will take the heart of stone out of your flesh and give you a heart of flesh. Ezekiel 36.26

You want God's help? You have to admit to your mistakes. You can start by humbly offering a sincere prayer: "My God, I want a new heart. Take away my heart of stone and give me a heart of flesh. Show me how to behave. Help me to be the person You want me to be."

If you don't agree with what we're saying and would prefer to continue doing things your way, then you can forget it. Not even God can help those who refuse to renounce their heart of stone. But if you sincerely want to surrender and allow God to mould you into the person you need to be, He will help you destroy your heart of stone, restore your marriage and erase any thoughts of divorce.

But don't assume that you can now sit idly by while God does all the work. That is not how things work. God requires a partnership before He will act. He's going to help you do what you cannot do, but your effort is necessary. God will give you the tools to destroy your hardened heart. Grinding stones is not an easy job, but we're going to tell you what to do, and not to do, to achieve this.

Recognising our mistakes is painful, but this is where you have to start. Go through the pain now, and experience relief for the rest of your life. The alternative is to cling to your mistakes and sink with them, suffering for years to come. Which do you prefer?

TASK:

Have a talk with your spouse. Ask him or her this question: What makes me a difficult person to live with? Write down the answers and then switch roles. If your spouse doesn't want to do this exercise, think about the main complaints he or she commonly makes about you, and write them down. Remember: The smartest person takes the first step towards change. Pay attention to the rules: Paper, pen, listen and write. You are not allowed to disagree or defend yourselves. There should be zero emotions during this task. Simply explore the other person's point of view, even if you disagree. The important thing is to understand what he or she is feeling.

Don't take anything personally. Remember to stuff your emotions away before starting this task. Even if you do not agree, take a deep breath and continue. Don't attack your partner's character, and try to express yourself in a way that focuses on the problem. Then protect this list with your life. Do not lose it. Show your spouse that you're taking this seriously.

If you put your emotions to the side and remain focused, this list will hold precious information that will be useful in your making changes. This is not a competition. Don't worry about whose list is longer. What matters is that you put everything out on the table. Another crucial point: After this exercise, you should no longer point out these items to your partner, or demand that they work on an item on the list. You are only responsible only for your part.

Roll up your sleeves and get to work. Today you start breaking stones.

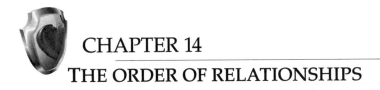

CHAPTER 14
THE ORDER OF RELATIONSHIPS

Basic mathematics teaches us that "factors can be multiplied in any order and the product is always the same". This always works in multiplication, but it doesn't always apply to our lives. In a marriage, the order of factors changes the final product a great deal. After an Olympic competition, the winners are placed on the podium in winning order and receive awards according to their final positions. No one would give the gold medal to the third place runner, or bronze to the first place runner, but you may be doing this at home because you simply do not know who deserves the three positions on your marriage podium.

THIS REFEREE IS NEVER BIASED

God clearly states that He should come first in our lives. This is not egotism on His part. He knows what He's doing. He knows people and realises that chaos is inevitable when this rule is not followed. When you don't put God in first place, you will naturally occupy that position. And when you put yourself first in life... let others get out of the way! No one can stand you. You make all sorts of mistakes and will end up a selfish bore, like we mentioned in the previous chapter. Your heart hardens and you let your marriage go down the drain. God suggests that we put Him in first place so that we have a referee in life. Having a referee is essential, especially in marriage.

Without a doubt, I can say my marriage was saved because we both put God in first place. If it were not for that, I'm not sure we'd still be together. Marriage is the union of two completely different people—so it's only natural that there will be times you disagree, in spite of your love. One will say A, the other will say B, and both will be sure they are right. How can you solve this problem? There is only one solution: Have a referee, a judge. His impartial law will make the final decision.

There have been times when I had to back off from my reasoning, as did Cristiane, and allow God's reasoning to prevail. It was no longer what I wanted, what I thought was right or what she thought was right, but what God said and determined should be done. You can't imagine how much simpler this makes a couple's life; it solves so many problems.

Isn't this what Jesus established when He was asked about the most important commandment of all? *You shall love the Lord your God with all your heart, with all your soul, and with all your mind. This is the first and great commandment. And the second is like it: You shall love your neighbour as yourself*[12]. God first, your neighbour second—in that order. But who is your closest neighbour? Isn't it your husband or wife?

When we worked in Texas, we came across many people who showed a shallow spirituality. Many of these people attended our marriage course and were amazed by it. They would tell all their friends about it, and saw great changes in their relationships. And yet, in many cases, those changes were not enough to permanently transform their marriages. Although the great majority of the attendees belonged to a church, since most people in Texas are evangelical Christians, they did not have a real relationship with God. There is a big difference. Having a real relationship with God, treating Him like the most important person in our lives and

---

[12] Matthew 22:36-40

proving it with our actions, has nothing to do with religion or religious practices. I like the way my colleague, Marcus Vinicius, explained during one of our courses how couples should look to God:

When you look to God, try to remove all religious prejudices. View God as righteousness; see Him as truth. Not your truth, nor your spouse's truth, but the truth that's going to help both of you overcome your problems together. This has nothing to do with religion, but with the important values that every human being needs and appreciates. It is not intelligent to deny Him first place in your life. If what you think is fair is different from what your partner thinks is fair, whose opinion will prevail in the end? Only the righteousness that comes from above, the perfect righteousness, can bring true balance and justice into your relationship—And without justice there can be no love.

If you have no higher authority to mediate your conflicts, you will end up stuck in your own opinions. Who's right? She thinks she's right, and he thinks he is, but thinking doesn't necessarily mean or prove anything. That's why every sport has rules and every country has a constitution. You can't show up at work in shorts unless you're a lifeguard or work for Google. In other words, there has to be discipline or else things will become a mess. Why would it be any different in marriage? You may not like the rules, but they exist to help regulate our relationships with people.

If there were no referees on a football field, the game would never end, no fouls would be called and confusion would reign. Both teams would want to play until they won and would never agree on anything. Players frequently badmouth referees, but the teams (and fans) understand that they are necessary to maintain order. Likewise, when we place God first in our lives, He becomes the Judge in our marriage. It's well worth having Him around for those times when we're unable to reach an agreement...

This is when we search for God's view on the situation and then obey His decision with confidence, knowing that it'll be for the best. After all, He is not a biased referee. It's very difficult to have a happy marriage when we ignore the rules of the game as established by God.

AND THE SILVER MEDAL GOES TO...

After the gold medal is awarded to God, there you are with a silver medal in your hand... You wish you could put it around your own neck, your son's little neck, or you mother's. But the proper answer lies in the Bible passage that cites the creation of marriage. Do you remember this passage?

Therefore a man shall leave his father and mother and be joined to his wife, and they shall become one flesh. Genesis 2.24

Marriage came with this rule in the instruction manual. For man (and woman) to get married, he must first leave his father and mother, leave the nest. If we have to leave our parents, the most influential people in our lives, do we really have to ask about siblings, friends and our ex-girlfriend's Facebook page? "And they shall become one flesh" indicates the beginning of a new family. When you get married, you leave your family of origin and form a new family. Your new family is your spouse. Your parents, siblings and other family members become your relatives, as shown in the following diagram.

Your original family becomes relatives after marriage

I am not saying that parents and siblings are no longer important, but you need to move to your own nest and start your new family. Clear boundaries are necessary to maintain a healthy relationship with all concerned. If this line is not clear, there will be unwelcome interference.

A common mistake of newlyweds and their relatives is that they're not seen as a separate family until they have a child. When the first child arrives, it's common to hear "Now our family's complete", but that overlooks the fact that the family was complete from the moment they got married. Having children is a choice, not a mandatory step in a relationship. (And please, never make the decision to have a child as a means to solving a problem between you and your spouse, or filling a void. It'll never work.)

Man joins his wife and they become one flesh. A new family is born, completed and sealed, with no room for interference from third parties. Besides God, nothing and nobody should take precedence over your husband or wife. If you are one flesh, when you take care of your spouse you're taking care of your own body. By prioritising your partner, the most important part of you, you are prioritising yourself.

Unfortunately, many women think it's this kind of relationship they should have with their children, who are blood of their blood. After you've carried a baby inside your body for nine months, you feel connected to him or her for the rest of their lives—even more than your child's father. But your child will grow up and want to live his own life and form his own family. Becoming one flesh with someone who will inevitably leave your home in a number of years makes no sense. This is a recipe for frustration and suffering. Children need to experience the solid base of their parents' marriage in order to form their own base in the future.

The strength of a relationship is in a couple's bond, and the only way to have a strong bond is by establishing proper priorities. Those who put work above their spouses, create a rift in the relationship. And yet it's so easy to let other things or people come before your husband or wife, even when you would not verbally admit it. If anybody asks, you're likely to say that your spouse is more important, but your actions prove who, or what, truly comes first.

The importance we place on a person or thing is measured by the time we devote to it and by what we do, not by what we say. We need to observe our actions. Who has received the most, or better part of our time, effort, attention and thoughts? Your spouse should receive preferential treatment and the best of your time. If most of it is spent at your mother's house or with co-workers, you are exposing your marriage to great risk and leaving it without protection. You need to pay close attention to this every single day. Stop and weigh your actions.

I'd say *I love you* to my wife, but the way I ignored and failed to take care of her cancelled out my words. My actions proved to her that the most important thing in my life was my job. In my case, it is tricky because my job is serving God. It's so easy to get confused and assume that everything related to God should come before my wife, since He is in first place, above her. But don't confuse God with the work of God.

Though I worked as a pastor, and served God, I should not have put the work of God before my wife. He makes this clear when He speaks about pastors, bishops and every other servant of God, saying that they have to have a good marriage and take care of their families first, so that afterwards they can take care of the church. God is not contradicting Himself when He says a pastor should take care of his family first. He will still occupy first place because the work of God is not God. What a value He puts on marriage! He doesn't want you to do His work if you are not a good example at home or fail to care for your spouse as the first sheep in your flock. In fact, marriage serves as a gauge to measure our relationship with God. If I am close to God, I will do very well in my marriage. If I'm not doing well in my marriage, I must be distant from God.

For a marriage to work, husband and wife have to care for each other more than for any other person or thing. If this doesn't happen, there is no real marriage. When she occupies the correct spot on the podium, a wife feels honoured to have been chosen above all other women. If she's pushed off to the side, she'll be bitter and unhappy. An unhappy woman makes for an unhappy home, and let's face it, that is not something you want. When a husband occupies the correct spot, he feels respected for being allowed to care for his wife as if she were his own body.

Now that you know these things and are one flesh, remove anyone else from the equation. The closeness that you have with your spouse should be similar to being glued together, inseparable. There can be no other person between you, not even your children.

Of course, there are rare exceptions. If your husband is a drug user, his behaviour creates risks for the entire family. In this case, you and the children, if you have any, become the priority because your husband's actions put your family's safety at risk. In this case, a temporary separation might be needed so that he can seek treatment. Of course, if God were first in his life, he would not be addicted to a drug, but that's a topic for a whole different book.

With first and second place duly filled by God and your spouse, third place goes to the rest of humanity: Children, relatives, friends and so forth. Let's get organised.

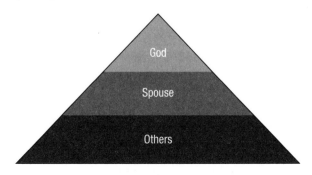

The order of relationships as determined by God

WHAT TO DO ABOUT NOSY PEOPLE?

It's not easy to draw the line with friends and relatives, especially when they had a habit of intruding before you got married. But before you start complaining about your family, stop inviting the intrusions. When you share your problems with friends and relatives, you're giving them permission to judge your spouse, make biased judgments and treat your life as if it were theirs. If you expose your life to your relatives as though it were a soap opera, you can't complain afterwards.

What should you do when nosy relatives invade your relationship? Fighting and throwing a fit are useless. Use your head. When people from your spouse's family of origin are the invaders, understand that relatives will always be relatives. It's not smart to attack them because you'll be attacking your partner's origins and creating an even bigger problem. Then they will see *you* as the invader who is trying to break them apart. The ideal thing to do is treat them the best you can and work on winning them over.

Cut evil at its roots and don't take things personally. For example, often the root behind a mother-in-law's bickering with her son's wife is insecurity. If you treat your mother-in-law well, clearly communicate that you are not her rival and that your goal is to make her son the happiest man in the world, you will make her feel more secure and less prone to give you problems. She should view you as her ally, someone to love and respect, never as an enemy. Learn to love your mother-in-law, even if it feels like Mission Impossible at the moment. If you've got this far in this book, you know it's not impossible. Remember Dian Fossey and the gorillas?

If relatives from your family of origin commonly interfere in your marriage, learn to prioritise your new family and show it by your actions. Be polite, don't intentionally hurt anyone, but establish clear boundaries so that relatives get the message that your family is sacred ground. Let them know that when they criticise your spouse, they're criticising you. Whoever loves you will have to learn to love your spouse as well, because you are now one.

When a couple decides to help a relative with financial problems, there is great potential for conflict. And yet, if you discuss things beforehand and reach an agreement, the problem should be taken care of. Couples need to be balanced and prioritise their needs, so that they can help those in need.

We know a couple who went through serious financial problems. They got into debt early in their marriage. Three years into the marriage, they were struggling to pay off the debt. At the time, the wife was concerned about her mother who was overdue on some of her bills, had an emotional talk with her husband and got him to take out a loan to help her. She had already decided the matter before speaking to her husband and would not consider any alternatives... good old emotional blackmail. With no room to manoeuvre, the husband gave in. And so, her attitude not only increased their debt load, but also caused wear and tear on their relationship. The husband felt less of a husband when he saw how little his wife prioritised the needs of their new family and paying off their debt.

Many couples do the right thing in the wrong order. It's not wrong to help your family of origin, as long as it's done at the right time and in the right way, and as long as you're not inconsiderate of your partner. If it makes your partner feel uncomfortable, you'll only create more problems.

Cristiane:
I'll never forget what my father said to me at the altar, during my wedding ceremony: "From now on no more running to mum and dad. Your problems will have to be resolved between you and Renato." Out of all he said that night, this is what was most striking to me. I think it was because I was still very young and very attached to my family.

His hard, direct words caused me to think about the new order of priorities I now had because of marriage. Renato was my family now, and I was his. Our parents became our relatives. The problems we had in the beginning of our marriage stayed between us. This isn't easy, especially for us women, who tend to want to say what we feel...

It's not hard to understand the concept of how we have to let go of our old family when we start a new one, but even so, this is a major problem among many couples today. This wasn't the case many years ago. The goal of marriage was to form a family. In fact, unmarried women were looked down upon by society and their own families.

At the time, many people got married even though they had no feelings for each other. It was their duty to get married, and that was it. You didn't always love the person you were marrying. But many couples who got married without feelings for each other, developed true love over time because they decided that they were now a family and they should start acting like one. In other words, act like a person who loves your husband or wife and you will become a couple. And if a couple puts each other first, they'll be a family and no one will be able to come between them.

TASK:

What adjustments do you need to make to establish the correct order in your relationship? Write down what you will do, especially what you will do differently, to make your spouse feel like the most important person in the world for you, after God.

/BulletproofMarriage

Post: I just corrected the order of my relationships. #Bulletproofmarriage

@BulletproofMate

Tweet: I just corrected the order of my relationships. #BulletproofMarriage @BulletproofMate

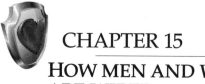

CHAPTER 15

HOW MEN AND WOMEN ARE WIRED

Before beginning this chapter, I did some quick research into how different men and women's minds are. I stopped writing for a minute, left my office and went into the bathroom where Cristiane was blow-drying her beautiful hair while listening to music on her iPad. Without letting her know what I was doing, I walked over to the sink and washed my hands. I looked at her in the mirror and asked: What are you thinking about?

With no hesitation whatsoever, she replied: "I'm thinking about how Rafaela hasn't posted the movie review from last week on my blog yet. I have to send her an e-mail. I was also thinking about how this would be a good song to use on The Love School TV programme, but there's probably no official video of it on YouTube since it's such an old song. But I was thinking... production could probably use behind-the-scenes footage from the show to make a clip for this song. And talking about the production team, when I went into their room yesterday, I noticed they need more chairs. One of them has to work standing up. Oh, and I was also thinking about how dry my hair is. I'd like to pay someone to blow-dry my hair instead of doing it myself. "

"Anything else?" I dared ask.

"No, that's all."

That's all... my wife had been thinking about five different things and that song hadn't even finished playing. I was only thinking about one thing: How am I going to write this chapter!

One fact that most couples ignore is the difference between the sexes and how it affects their relationship. Men deal with their wives as if they were dealing with another man. Women speak to their husbands as if they were women. Every one of these interactions opens up a new can of worms.

When you understand these differences, everything changes without anything actually changing. Things change because you begin to understand that your spouse is not doing this or that because he's a bad person or because she wants to irritate you. They're just being who they are: A man or a woman. They're not mean; you're just very different from each other.

Cristiane:

"If I were in his shoes, I wouldn't have done that." This is what I occasionally thought about Renato. I was constantly criticising men when they showed a lack of sensitivity to others. I would walk into a building carrying a bunch of bags, one heavier than the other, and men would just stand there and not even think of helping me. And I'd think, "I wish men would act more like gentlemen!"

I was constantly comparing myself to Renato, and because we were two very different people, you can just imagine the thoughts that ran through my mind. He didn't even notice my new clothes, whereas my girlfriends noticed them right away. "How can you do that?" I would ask, but he couldn't understand why these things were so important to me. It was as though we were from two different planets! Then one day, I realised I was being unfair by wanting him to think like me. He's a man.

This is a terrible mistake that many of us make. We want other people to think like us. This happens even with things that have to do with taste. Someone likes something different, we think it's horrible, but does it matter? Does it matter whether or not I like another woman's hair colour when her hair is not mine? But this is what we do with our partners. We criticise them for not always thinking or doing things our way.

In the battle of who does it best, nobody wins. On the other hand, it fills a marriage with friction. I wanted him to show the same sensitivity to me that I showed to him, and he wanted me to be just as tough as he was. He wanted me to be a man and I wanted him to be a woman.

Of course, at first we didn't notice that. I never imagined that I would ever ask my husband to be a woman! But if I had made a list of everything I wanted him to be, it would have been a male version of me. As if I would ever put up with myself!

This is the pure, unadulterated truth. Ask any woman to describe her "ideal man" and she'll describe another woman...

But men and women differ in many ways. Genetically, the 23rd chromosome determines a person's gender. Physically, male and female bodies are obviously different. But one of the most distinct differences is in their brains.

On average, a male brain is 10% bigger than a female brain and has 4% more cells. But before the men start bragging about having bigger brains, research also shows that female brains have more nerve cells and connectors, which allow the brain to be more efficient and effective. What this means is that, in general, men tend to perform tasks that use the left side of the brain, which is the logical, rational side. Women, on the other hand, tend to use both sides simultaneously because of their ability to rapidly transfer information between left and right sides of the brain. The result is that men tend to be more focused on things, systems and solving problems, while women tend to be creative and more attuned to how everyone around them is feeling. Studies acknowledge that there are some exceptions, and that it is possible for a man to have a "more feminine" brain and vice versa—which has nothing to do with their sexual preference. Don't worry! This simply means that some men are more emotional and some women are more rational—but they are not the majority.

In Louann Brizendine's book *The Female Brain*, she explains how both brains are very different, from the crib. Baby girls grow into little girls who love to make friends and socialise with other girls. They even notice when things are not going well at home. But when it comes to baby boys, who grow into big boys, things are not the same. They want to play, and if they hurt someone in the process, that's okay, no problem. They love challenge and adventure. At a very young age, he is already a conqueror and she is already a loving companion.

ONE BOX FOR EACH AND EVERY THING

In my opinion, Mark Gungor spells out these differences the best. He explains that the male brain is made up of boxes. In a man's brain there's a box for everything: One for his car, one for his job, one for you, one for his children, one for his mother-in-law somewhere in the basement, sealed and labelled "Danger! Do not touch"... And one very important detail is that these boxes never touch each other. Whenever a man wants to discuss a subject, he pulls out the one box that has to do with that particular topic, opens it and discusses only what's inside that box. When he's done, he closes the box and puts it back in its place being very, very careful not to touch any other box.

And there's more: Women, pay close attention!

Inside a man's brain there is a little box that most women are unaware of. This box has nothing in it. In fact, it's called "the nothing box". Out of all of the boxes, this little box is our favourite. Whenever he has a chance, he'll run to his nothing box every time. This is why men are able to engage in activities that require virtually zero brain activity for hours on end, such as playing video games, fishing or sitting in front of the TV changing channels, not actually watching anything. If you let us, when we're stressed out or under pressure we'll automatically gravitate to our nothing box.

Women have a hard time understanding this because they just can't stop thinking about things. Whenever a woman sees her husband in this vegetative, zombie-like state, she can't help but come over and ask:

—What are you thinking about?

After waking up from nothing-world, he'll reply:

—Nothing.

—You must be thinking about *something*. It's impossible to think about nothing.

—I already told you, I wasn't thinking about anything.—He insists.

—No, you're lying. You just don't want to tell me. That's the problem, you never open up to me.

Every man has had this conversation and fears it because he knows it's not going to end well. No matter what he says, she's not going to believe him. If he says he wasn't thinking about anything, she doesn't believe that's humanly possible. If he pretends he was thinking about something just to get her off his back, she's going to suspect that he's not being totally honest with her (not realising that she's hit the nail on the head... he really wasn't thinking about that).

What she does not understand is that when men are stressed out, or under pressure at work, their way of relaxing is to run to their nothing box. He wants to be left alone. He doesn't want to speak. He just wants to be quiet for a while. The last thing he wants to do is talk about his problems and frustrations. A man will only tell another man his problems when he thinks that man can help him solve them. Otherwise, he just keeps trying to process things quietly inside his head.

But when a woman is stressed out, she has to speak to someone—not necessarily for advice—because she will literally explode if she doesn't talk about things...

A BALL OF WIRES

If a man's brain is made up of a bunch of boxes, a woman's brain is like a ball of yarn, a tangled web of wires. Everything is connected to everything else: The car is connected to her job, which is connected to her children, who are connected to her mother, who is connected to the leak in the bathroom... Everything's tied together and nothing happens by chance. And emotion is the energy flowing through these wires. That's why a woman tends to remember everything, like the details of a conversation her husband swears never happened. That's because whenever you link an event to an emotion, that event will be burned into your memory and you'll never forget it. Men also have this ability, they just don't use it that often because they couldn't care less about the small details. But women remember every single little thing...

When a woman is stressed out and needs someone to talk to, the man will mistakenly think he has to solve her problems for her. She might say:

—You know what happened today? Pamela took all the credit for the work I did.

—Who's Pamela?—he asks, completely disengaged from what's going on.

—Honey, she's one of my co-workers at the office!—she tells him for the 20th time. And continues—When she handed our boss the project I killed myself over these last two weeks, he signed it and assumed she'd done it all on her own.

—Well, you have to tell her that she can't do that. Or find a way to let your boss know that you were the one who put the whole thing together. Or just let it go and stop worrying about it.

Her husband thinks he's just solved things by giving her some great advice. The truth is he's just made her feel like an idiot, that she has no idea what to do in this situation. She doesn't need advice, all she wants is someone to listen to her. She needs to talk because her mind is being attacked by frustration and with this and that thought. What her husband needs to do right away is shut his mouth and listen. If he doesn't have the sense and self-control to do this, she's going to go to her mother, sister, friend, or even worse, to Richard at the office. If a woman understands her husband's brain and he understands hers, the two can make allowances for this male/female differences and will avoid irritating and frustrating each other.

IS HE DEAF?

Because of their differences, women tend to be great multi-taskers, and naturally find themselves doing a number of things at once. Men tend to be great single-taskers, and like to concentrate on one thing at a time. Once again, this can be a source of annoyance. Women often blame men for not paying attention to what they say. For example, a husband may be on the sofa reading the newspaper while the wife is preparing dinner, keeping track of their son while he does his homework and talking on the phone, all at the same time. She hangs up and says to her husband, "My niece's birthday party is this coming Saturday. We have to be there around 3 o'clock." He mumbles from the living room, "Yeah, okay".

Fast-forward to Saturday and he notices his wife getting ready for something, and asks, "Where are you going?" She answers in frustration, "You always forget about everything, don't you? You never pay attention to what I say." The reality is that he was totally focused on reading his newspaper when she spoke to him. This doesn't mean that he doesn't care about her. It's simply the way his brain works. If you want to reduce these types of misunderstandings, make sure your husband is completely focused on you when you talk to him. In other words, make sure he's looking straight at you and not doing anything else. If not, then wait for the right moment to tell him.

The differences between the sexes dictate much more than a few little rules of coexistence and communication. Over the centuries, men and women have been naturally programmed to expect very specific things from each other. Unfortunately, today more than ever, these expectations are not always clearly understood. We will now attempt to explain how they developed, what they are and how to satisfy them.

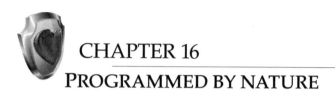

CHAPTER 16
PROGRAMMED BY NATURE

From the very beginning of time, the physical, genetic and mental makeup of men and women created social and cultural differences. A man's physical strength, skill with weapons, navigating abilities and competitive nature made him a natural provider and protector of the family. The inherent characteristics of a woman made her a natural carer for the children and home organiser.

For thousands of years their roles have been different, yet clear and specific. The routine of a typical couple was pretty much like what I describe below.

Before sunrise, a man would leave his house with weapons slung over his shoulder to hunt alone or in a group, and risk his life to bring food back home. A woman stayed home, waiting anxiously for his return at the end of the day, not only with food, but unharmed. He was her hero, who risked his life for her and their children. While hunting, men did not make great use of their verbal skills because any small sound could scare the game away. They had to speak in hushed tones and at times communicate with gestures. They could not be afraid to kill—animal or man—when attacked.

On the other hand, a woman stayed home with her children and neighbours, forcing her to hone her communication skills, which were already first-rate. As the organiser and nurse of the family, she developed an expertise at facial expressions and problem solving, always alert to the physical and emotional states of others. She became an architect of relationships, the glue that held her family and community together.

You may now understand why men developed an unemotional disposition, are not as good at the inborn female gift of "reading people's moods", and are less talkative and more direct with their words.

In addition to the things they did to hold the home together, women were cherished for their almost divine ability to bear children. She carried within her body the seed of life. For this reason, a man protected and valued her. She, in turn, respected him as the natural leader of the family and appreciated him for risking his life on a daily basis to guarantee the family's survival.

Because of all these things, men and women's roles were clearly defined. There was no argument nor competition. Each knew his or her role in life and neither was tempted to look down on the other. It remained this way for thousands of years. Through many centuries these roles hardly varied at all. Men have traditionally been the providers and protectors of the family, and women have been the caregivers of the home and the architects of the marriage relationship.

However, over the past 50 years, certain factors have caused this reality to change. We could cite many, but we will limit ourselves to only two major factors and their effects on marriage.

THE SWITCHING OF ROLES

Two social phenomena transformed the traditional concept of a man and woman's role in society: The Feminist Movement and the Industrial Revolution. It is beyond the scope of this book to go into detail about these two points. Feel free to do your own research if you feel the need. But for our purposes, here are the main points and why we care:

THE INDUSTRIAL REVOLUTION

Women started to leave the home for work, fairly timidly at first, in the mid-19th century. Changes in manufacturing and technology gave rise to the opening of factories, which led to job opportunities that had been non-existent for women up to that point. But over the last century, especially after World War II, women began to make a name for themselves in the job market. They proved themselves to be as capable as men in many professions. They earned equal rights and surpassed men in the number of students enrolled in universities. With the explosive growth in industry, technology, public service and health care, women are now an essential part of the global economy. With the added buying power of a woman, couples are able to afford much more than their parents and grandparents could. On top of that, the current materialistic culture—relentless advertising of products and goods that promise "happiness" to those who consume them—makes it practically impossible for a man of average or low income to support a family. He needs his wife's extra income. What this means is this: A woman is no longer simply the mother and wife who runs the household and welcomes her husband at the end of the day with a warm cake waiting in the oven. She is as equally active as her husband and earns as much or more than he does; and so she is strikingly different from a traditional woman. She has also become a hunter.

THE FEMINIST MOVEMENT

American feminist and social activist bell hooks[13] defines the essence of feminism as: "The struggle to end sexist oppression". I think everyone would agree that throughout history, men have caused women, and other men, to suffer great hardship. And so, the validity of the struggle

---

[13] She intentionally does not capitalize her name. Curiously, at age 60 she still remains unmarried.

 178

for women's rights cannot be denied. But just as feminists have made great strides in gender equality, they have also engendered a certain hatred or dislike for men. In general, feminism encourages women to view men as oppressors, as an enemy who's ready to oppress them the first chance he gets. Though this is true in some cases, this generalisation leads women to reject the traditional role of men as breadwinners and protectors; they fear it would be an acknowledgement that they are beneath men. Waving the women's rights flag also creates confusion between *equal rights* and gender equality. It's when women view men as their equals in terms of gender that numerous conflicts arise, especially in marriage.

I'd like to be very clear about this: I am completely in favour of equal rights for both sexes. But when we say that men and women have the same nature and needs, we make a grave mistake that will have serious consequences in people's love lives. It's one thing to have equal rights, and another to assume you have the same roles. Men and women have always had equal rights in God's eyes, since He didn't create one to be better than the other. But the roles they were assigned are altogether different. The problem begins when a woman wants to fulfil a man's role in a marriage and family.

These two factors can be summarised in one phrase: The rise of women. As a result, their roles are no longer as clear, distinct and specific as they used to be. For the first time in human history, men have an identity crisis.

WHO AM I? WHERE AM I?

Who's this female "hunter" at my side? Men haven't adjusted to this new scenario, and the changes we have just discussed are behind a large number of marriage problems. Women have become more independent and less likely to involve husbands in their decisions. They butt heads because they feel they "can" do this or that on their own. Men in turn feel intimidated by the growth in women's power, and withdraw. In some cases, men start to feel less than women. His traditional firmness turns to indecision, and he does anything to please his wife and keep the peace. She in turn gets frustrated with his lack of initiative and ends up taking the lead. This vicious cycle continues, and in the end, she takes on his role and he takes on hers.

The result is that a rise in feminism over the last 50 years coincides with an increase in divorce. How can something so good for women, be so bad for relationships?

We are not suggesting that the advancements that women have made are bad, and we do not want society to go back to the way it used to be. We just want to highlight the fact that though society has changed, the basic needs of men and women have remained the same for thousands and thousands of years. Men are still men and women have not stopped being women. We were created this way. New rights and norms are not going to change our DNA. We are naturally programmed to be this way—we are made to expect certain things from our spouses.

Men and women can grow and evolve as much as they want. There is no inherent problem in a woman earning more money than a man, or in a man washing dishes and changing diapers. What both sexes need to understand is *how to meet each other's basic needs.* Let's hold on to the progress and advancements of women, but at the same time rescue the original values and principles that make for a happy marriage.

Cristiane:

I'm in favour of women's rights. I, too, like to achieve big things. The problem is knowing how to act towards our men when it comes to these changes in society.

My parents have been married for more than 40 years and their mindset is very different from the couples who get married today. When my father married my mother, he thought about working hard to support her. Today, many men no longer have that concern. Women also work and often may even support their husbands. In the past, this would have been humiliating for a man because it made him look weak. If he took a girl from her parents' home, he had an obligation to care for her and provide everything she needed.

Meanwhile, her duty was to take care of her husband, their home and raise their children. She took pleasure in doing this, which is something we do not often see these days. Modern women do not always find pleasure in caring for their husbands, let alone the house. If he's hungry, he can cook himself something to eat. Her children spend most of their time in school and sports so she has more time for her career and other interests. When she arrives home, she doesn't want to have the hassle of cooking or cleaning anything, so she gets upset when her husband leaves a pair of shoes in the middle of the room. What was not a problem in the past has now become the cause of an argument.

Men and women were not made to compete with each other. We are very different, and our differences were meant to add to our spouse's life, not to be used as ammunition to put them down.

The media contributes to this disaster by helping to put men down. Have you ever noticed that most comedies and other types of movies cast men as the weaker characters, who are afraid of women, do everything wrong, have no say and inspire no confidence—while women are intelligent, know what they want, do everything right and support the family?

This brainwashes people into thinking: Men are weak, women are strong, men are fools, women are smart. The result is that children no longer respect their fathers, wives don't respect their husbands and men get the short end of the stick. Wives accuse men of being incapable of supporting the family and children feel disappointed in their fathers, and tell themselves that they'll never get married.

We've just painted you the picture of a family in the 21st century. If society does not value a man's role in the family, men will not value a woman's role, and what happens next is inevitable: No one appreciates anyone else, it's every person for him or herself—overblown selfishness every day of their lives.

If you want to have a happy, long-lasting marriage, you cannot follow the rules of today's culture. You must paddle against the current and create your own culture within your relationship. Cristiane and I have our culture, and we've determined that nothing harmful will be allowed to enter. This is why we are able to maintain values and principles that protect our closeness—and we do not forget to fulfil each other's basic needs, which are pre-determined by our different natures.

Do you know what these needs are? Let's understand a little bit more about them.

BASIC NEEDS

We are programmed by human nature to have certain needs that have to be met. The most basic are food, water, clothing and shelter. Deprive a man of these things and he will start behaving like an animal. This can be seen when natural disasters strike a city. All of a sudden, people find themselves without food, water, shelter and safety. If emergency services do not respond quickly and help these people, they switch into survival mode and become aggressive. The desperate search for food, water and shelter can cause people to act like cavemen. When people are deprived of their basic needs, they react in primitive ways.

Minutes before a disaster occurs, most people are concerned with insignificant things: Is one pant leg shorter than the other, should I paint my bedroom beige or white, should I upgrade my phone? etc. After a horrible tragedy, nobody cares about those things. They're concerned about saving their lives. What they saw as a "necessity" a few minutes ago is now insignificant compared to basic things like water, food and blankets. People who've never stolen a thing, never attacked anyone or broken the law, are now capable of doing those very things. It's instinctual. So then, how can we best contain this animalistic behaviour? By fulfilling their basic needs.

There is something else that's important to know:

You can't question a person's basic needs. The only thing you can do is meet them.

It's not a crime to be hungry. You're not an evil person for wanting a good night's sleep. Being thirsty is not against the law. No one should be made to feel guilty for wanting a proper home. People who could meet these needs and don't are the ones who are evil.

Now, apply this logic to your relationship. Men and women also have basic needs that need to be met, because of their male and female make-up. Certain things need to be done for a marriage to work. Okay, your husband may not be as romantic as Robert Redford, your wife may not be the image of perfection from the latest Hollywood hit—and yet, you should provide the essentials to each other, at the very least.

The basic needs of a man and woman are extremely important. If they're not met, your husband or wife will act irrationally. And at that point it's useless to criticise or wonder "why is he like that?" or "why is she acting that way?" The best thing you can do about your partner's basic needs is meet them. There's no discussing a person's needs. When you're starving, the only useful thing you can do is eat.

When you buy a pet, the first thing you do is find out what it eats, drinks, likes and dislikes—even before you take it home. You don't argue with the salesman or try to change the animal's eating habits. If you want a happy pet, all you have to do is meet its needs, no matter how much work you have to put into that. If you want a happy husband or wife, find out what his or her basic needs are and meet them. Don't argue about them, just meet them.

WANTS AND COMPARISONS

A clarification: We're talking about basic needs, not wants, whims or dreams. A warning for women: True love is not about romance and Hollywood kisses. Women often make the big mistake of comparing real men to men in movies. A married woman once left a comment on one of our YouTube videos describing her ideal man:

> ... I like a man that takes care of himself, knows how to express his feelings, and is romantic like Brad Pitt or Tom Cruise. But he has to be a gentleman like James Bond and a provider and protector like Conan the Barbarian. I think the ideal man is like that vampire from Twilight. And I also like that man from "Gone with the Wind", and the one from "Dancing in the Rain"... Oh, I don't know, maybe a little bit of each one. I also like the Samurais...

My advice for this wife was pretty simple: Stop watching movies!

The illusion of love that Hollywood creates causes lots of marriages to fail. It's scripted, practised, directed and produced, and real life cannot compete with it. In real life, that soap opera hunk has been married three or four times, has an unhappy love life, and may even beat his wife. We can't live out reality based on fantasy.

One of the worst things you can do is compare your spouse to someone else, anyone—real or imaginary. This will kill your marriage. If you compare your husband to TV husbands, get ready for frustration.

The same applies to men. The same thing will happen when you drift off into the plague of pornography. Putting aside the moral aspect of this subject, the fact is that many men are no longer sexually excited by their wives as a result of this addiction. They only find "pleasure" in porn and masturbation. Real life intimacy with his wife no longer matters. These men stop being the men their wives need, experience frustration from comparing their wives to the women on the videos they watch, and find themselves living in a fantasy world. Their marriages have an expiry date.

No woman likes to be compared in this way. It's humiliating for her to know that her husband is only satisfied by these types of images. In the end, she doesn't get as excited as him by it and both are robbed of total intimacy. A man who depends on this kind of stimulation demoralises his wife, and sends her the clear message that she is not enough for him—the opposite of her most basic need.

PART IV

BULLETPROOFING IT

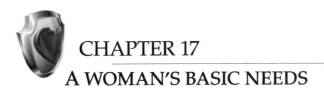

CHAPTER 17

A WOMAN'S BASIC NEEDS

What are the basic needs of a woman? We can sum it up in one sentence: To be valued and cared for. This is how the divine intelligence defines a husband's primary responsibility to his wife:

Husbands, go all out in your love for your wives, exactly as Christ did for the church—a love marked by giving, not getting... And that is how husbands ought to love their wives. They're really doing themselves a favour—since they're already "one" in marriage. (Ephesians 5.25,28 – MSG)

Notice the comparison in the very beginning of this passage between a husband's love for his wife and Christ's love for the Church. God's love is used as an example to be followed. The love we have for our wives should not be modelled after movies, books, parents, relatives or friends. The Author of marriage pointed to the love of Jesus as a reference point for husbands. And what kind of love did He have? A love marked by selfless giving, sacrifice, care and renunciation—not emotion.

Men are then led to understand that loving their wives is the same as loving themselves. When I take care of Cristiane, I am actually taking care of myself. If I were to hurt her, I would be hurting myself. Do you remember that the two people in marriage "become one flesh"? Husbands should see their wives as an extension of themselves and refuse to neglect their needs.

A wife is a gift from God to her husband[14]. God created women for men, and the way men were made also complements women. If a husband rejects, mistreats, or abandons his wife, he is rejecting God's gift (the same is true for a wife who rejects her husband). When you belittle your wife by saying "women just want to spend money", or when you belittle your husband by saying "men are all the same", you are actually belittling God because He created both.

A wife is under her husband's care. The origin of the word husband stems from a word that means "Tiller of the ground". Being a husband therefore invokes the idea of caring for, helping to grow. And so the role of a married man is to be responsible for his wife, for everything that happens to her, and to care for her. This is true love. Love is much more than a feeling. It is action. The world says: "If you no longer have feelings for each other, you no longer love each other." This feeling-based love generates serial daters—they simply stop loving one person and go to the next, and then the next, etc. True love is not based on emotion, but on the care that a husband has for his wife and the commitment he has made to her.

APPRECIATE AND LOVE HER. BUT HOW?

A wife feels appreciated and loved when:

Her husband makes her feel secure—This is not simple physical and financial security, but *security* in every sense of the word. The dictionary defines secure as:

---

[14] Proverbs 18:22

Not subject to threat; certain to remain or continue safe and unharmed; protected against attack; feeling safe, stable, and free from fear or anxiety.[15]

A man can make a woman feel secure in several ways. One way is to be faithful to her. A basic need of a woman is to know that her husband will stay faithful to her when he goes to work or anywhere else. When a man flirts with other women, even when it's a result of his outgoing personality, he makes his wife feel insecure. His playful behaviour, which may invite inappropriate friendships with other women, may need to be toned down so that his wife can feel more secure.

Being irresponsible, immature, indecisive, temperamental, a big spender, or given to addictions will also make her feel insecure. Men want their wives to trust them, but their behaviour may be giving off the wrong message. A man may think that being loud, screaming and slamming doors proves that he's strong and decisive, and yet he's proving the complete opposite. If he can't control himself, how will he control his family or the situation? Show me an angry, volatile husband and I'll show you an insecure, undervalued, unloved wife.

When a woman feels unsafe, she erects walls to protect herself from harm. Her instincts tell her that she has to protect herself since her husband's not going to do it. This also creates a vicious cycle where he feels disrespected and steps away, and she feels obligated to make decisions, take initiative and fight for herself—all of which increases his feelings that she is disrespecting him.

A husband has to be balanced and sure of himself. To protect and care for his wife, he has to be strong, but in the right way. He can't be an addict nor can he be indecisive. He can't want something one minute and something else the next. If he's immature, irresponsible, and has

---

[15] Oxford Online Dictionary

no strong leadership skills, she is guaranteed to take the lead to ensure their survival... Men, time to wake up!

He listens to her—This is difficult for a man. Men usually find it a challenge to pay attention for long periods or to listen to details. They prefer to solve problems rather than hear about them. They are different from women when they get together. A woman already feels better just by venting to her girl friend. But to men, that's a waste of time. So you have another problem: You want your wife to share everything with you, but you don't want to listen to her. No wonder women confide in their friends more often than in their own husbands!

Husbands frequently get angry with their wives for sharing something private with another person. But what can she do when her husband doesn't care to hear what she has to say? She's wrong... but so is he. If no one listens to her at home, there's a great chance that she will open up to someone outside the home. This represents a serious danger. When a woman's basic needs are neglected, she's an easy target of the friendly, helpful Casanova at work who can spot a woman with unmet needs a mile away, and who gives married women what their husbands have no time to give: A listening ear. When these women aren't given the attention they need at home, they become easy candidates for emotional affairs.

Men: Open your ears. Pay attention to them, especially when they're opening up about their problems. Don't try to fix them, just listen. Like we previously explained, women handle stress differently from men. They have to talk and release all that's disturbing them inside. This does not mean that she needs your advice. Probably all she needs is to be reassured that you're on her side with listening and hugs.

A couple's intimacy begins with listening. If you have no conversations, intimacy levels are most probably very low, because it's not only about the physical act of sex. Intimacy goes far beyond that. One more tip for men: Stop what you're doing and pay attention when she's talking, and you'll avoid problems later on! Worse than not listening is to pretend that you're listening... If you are unable to pay attention at that moment, let her know, or else you'll run into problems later on.

I had to learn how to listen. I didn't like to listen or to explain details. When my wife asked, "How was your day?" the most I would say was, "It was good". That would be the end of the conversation. But this was killing our intimacy. So I began to involve her in my life and make her feel that she was a part of my day.

He makes her feel she's the only one—She has a need to feel she's the only one you care about romantically, out of all the women in the world. You chose her and she's the only one for you. You could have chosen any other woman, but you chose her. She comes before your mother, children, siblings and friends. If someone in your family doesn't like your wife, you should be ready to walk into that relative's house holding her hand, proving that she's important to you and that you'll defend her at all costs. If there's a woman at your job or in your circle of friends who makes your wife feel insecure, it's your responsibility to make her feel secure with your actions (not only your words). I know a husband who does this by practising a simple rule of thumb: Not giving any woman a ride home, out of respect for his wife. Imagine how this makes her feel? She must feel like the woman in this beautiful love letter, written by Graciliano Ramos to his future wife:

I have noticed a strange phenomenon lately: The women died. I think there was an epidemic among them. After December they began disappearing, disappearing, and now they are gone. True, I see people wearing skirts out there, but I'm not sure if they are women… They all died. And this is why I am so drawn to the sole survivor. (Love letters to Heloise)

A woman needs to feel she's the only one. She tends to be insecure by nature. Society adds to this by bombarding her with images of what it deems beautiful and ugly in a woman, always comparing her to its standards: The ideal body, hair, skin and clothes. You don't see the same attack on men because they usually don't care about their looks like women do. If a friend tells him he's developing a spare tire, they'll laugh about it together; if a friend said the same thing to her, that person would immediately be added to a blacklist...

This is why a woman never tires of asking her husband whether or not he thinks she's pretty or loves her. Men who don't understand the reasoning behind this are tempted to say something like: "I proved that I love you when I married you. If anything changes, I'll let you know." It seems obvious to you, but it is not that simple to her. Be careful how you talk to your wife, because this can also contribute to her insecurity.

She's always on your radar—A wife should always be on her husband's radar. He should always be conscious of how and where she is, who she's with, be attentive to her present concerns and to what she's doing or needs. His radar is usually directed at work, bills, his own projects and concerns. But even when his focus is on these things, from time to time he has to remember her and point his radar in her direction.

If you forget to think about her throughout the day, you will probably be greeted with an angry face when you arrive home. As her protector, you have to be aware of her every step, not because you want to spy on or control her, but because you want to be a good caretaker.

Many couples are heading for divorce because they've turned their radar away from each other. They no longer care about what the other does or where the other goes. They are indifferent towards each other. This is how love grows cold. Every relationship needs constant invest-

YOUR SHIELD AGAINST DIVORCE

ment. If he forgets about her because of a job or a new project, she will feel unappreciated and unloved. Many women live in jealousy not because their husbands cheat on them. The root cause is because they feel unappreciated.

When she gets sick, he expects her mother or friends to take care of her, when he is the one who should do that whenever possible. If she's starting a new project, it's his responsibility to find out how these projects are going. She's his responsibility. He cannot brush her to the side as if she were any other woman in the world.

A wife once told us that her husband never had time for her because of his job. So, with his consent, she decided to schedule a vacation three months in advance for them to go on. The week before the vacation he told her he wouldn't be able to go because of his job and that she'd have to go with a friend and her children. How do you think she felt when her husband put his job before her?

He makes her feel attractive—When a woman asks the question that every man dreads: "Do you think I'm fat?"—and she really is a bit overweight, you can't lie but you have to be diplomatic... Women need to feel attractive because they're up against a lot of competition: Magazines, newspapers, TV, women on the streets. The pressure is so intense that even models, the standards of beauty, often feel ugly. This need has been with her since her childhood. Girls love compliments, while boys don't really care. A woman needs praise. Don't be economical with it.

A man should use words that make her feel like a woman. When she feels ugly, her self-esteem is low and that's bad for both. When Cristiane puts on a few extra pounds, she asks me what I think and I always say, "That's great. Now there's a little more of you for me to love!"

There will always be a better-looking woman. There will never be a woman unanimously voted the most beautiful in the world. That's im-

195

possible. Beauty is very subjective. But in a husband's eyes his wife has to be the most beautiful woman in the world. He should only have eyes for her.

A husband needs to learn how to be his wife's lover, to see beyond her flaws. When he does this, his wife may be considered "ugly" by society, but she'll feel like the sexiest woman in the world because of how her husband makes her feel. A wise man will make his wife feel attractive.

Be caringly touched—Physical contact is essential for women. Many men find it difficult to show affection because of the way they were raised. Boys are expected to be strong as they grow up. They can't cry and they're not supposed to need anyone or anything. Women are a different story. Affection speaks volumes to them.

The level of physical affection between a man and a woman speaks louder than words. Over the years, many couples become distant, sleep in separate beds, live respectfully under the same roof like brother and sister, but they are indifferent to each other. When he wants to be physically intimate, he wakes her up at night and says, "Come on, babe". He wants her to be in the mood, and yet all day, week or month he has shown her no affection.

Sometimes a husband is ashamed to kiss or hug his wife in public. Others don't even like to hold hands. Women have these needs, especially when they're stressed out. And when he denies her this physical contact, she feels rejected. If you want your wife to feel appreciated, loved and crazy about you in bed, then know that this show of affection must always be present in your relationship, especially when you are not in bed.

Some women have no desire for physical affection because of past traumas and abuse. These cases should receive specialised help.

Cristiane:

I've always heard men say that women are complicated, we don't know what we want, that men have to stop being men in order to please us, but now you can understand where these myths came from. Okay, we're a bit complicated (okay, a lot), but that's because of our insecurities, which have already been explained. It's in our DNA. But this does not mean that we're hard to please. The problem is we are very different from men. What a man does not consider important, is very important for a woman, and vice-versa. It's easy to say that women don't know what they want. The real question is: Isn't this a good reason for men to stop criticising and pay more attention to us?

As a woman, I've overcome much insecurity, but unfortunately, because of nature, I have to continue to fight it on a daily basis. This is a female battle that never ends. So you showed your wife some affection one day last week, that doesn't mean you've done your part. Love and appreciation have to be shown through a combination of things you do.

When women love, they give themselves completely. In fact, they love to give themselves to people. They're always thinking of everyone else first, even those who dislike them. As her husband, you have much to gain from this feminine trait she has, but be careful: When a woman gets tired of giving, it may be too late for you to change.

TASK

FOR HUSBANDS:

Which of your wife's basic needs do you need to pay more attention to? What are you going to do about this from now on, so that she feels appreciated and loved?

FOR WIVES:

How can you help your husband understand your basic needs, without being demanding or imposing?

/BulletproofMarriage

Men, post: Now I know how to make my wife feel valued and cared for.
#Bulletproofmarriage

@BulletproofMate

Men, tweet: Now I know how to make my wife feel valued and cared for.
#BulletproofMarriage
@BulletproofMate

/BulletproofMarriage

Women, post: I am helping my husband understand what I need from him the most.
#Bulletproofmarriage

@BulletproofMate

Women, tweet: I am helping my husband understand what I need from him the most.
#BulletproofMarriage
@BulletproofMate

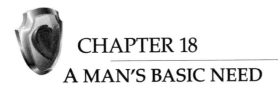

CHAPTER 18
A MAN'S BASIC NEED

Before we deal with the needs of men (a hint for women: It's not sex), let's refer back to our friends Adam and Eve. Earlier, we spoke about how God created them with shared authority over the earth. Nothing leads us to understand that he was more important than her, or that she was regarded as less than him. When God created Eve, His idea was to make a partner, a helper who was suitable for Adam[16]. Together, they would be happier and more capable than alone.

God gave her certain attributes that Adam did not have: Femininity, gentleness, sensuality, motherhood, heightened emotions, sweetness, magnetism, thoroughness, organisational skills... to name a few. The combination of these unique female qualities made Eve attractive to Adam. He wanted her by his side. When Adam saw Eve for the first time, he must have cried out: "That's worth a man leaving mum and dad for!"[17] Up to that moment, he'd not seen anything like her... There's no way he wanted to lose her. This is why every man has a natural desire to please a woman. When a man falls in love with a woman, he is bowled over by her. This can prove dangerous when a woman is un-

---

[16] Genesis 2:18,20
[17] Genesis 2:24

wise—not only for him, but for her too, since whatever happens to him will affect her. And that's exactly what happened.

Eve used her female charm and persuaded Adam to do what was wrong. Right away God realised that this power had to be controlled. If she was capable of this, and he was powerless to resist, something had to be done to balance things out. In other words, God recognised that Eve was stronger than Adam. Her ability to convince, combined with her attractiveness, put her in a position of great power and influence over her husband. This is why part of the curse that fell on her was: *...and he shall rule over you.*

This is when the idea of man being the head and woman being the body came into being. In other words, she would need to [insert scary soundtrack here] submit to him. Women, wait! Before you slam this book shut and angrily throw it in the rubbish bin, let me explain what this really means. Submitting to your husband most probably does not mean what you think. Let me take advantage of a woman's ability to add a special touch to things and allow my wife to disarm this time bomb...

THE POISONING OF A WORD

Cristiane:

Thanks a million, Honey!

Women, please read these words carefully because they were written to us:

Wives, understand and support your husbands in ways that show your support for Christ. The husband provides leadership to his wife the way Christ does to his church, not by domineering but by cherishing. So just as the church submits to Christ as he exercises such leadership, wives should likewise submit to their husbands. Ephesians 5:22-24 (MSG)

In the past, "submit" did not have the same negative connotation that it does today—thanks to the poison injected into this word by men and women who understand little about this concept. A concept that was positive and virtuous has become a swear word for many women. When you ask a woman in today's society to submit to her husband, in her mind you might as well ask her to become a Neanderthal. If people think that submission to a husband means being a doormat, allowing him to be chauvinistic to hit her on the head with a club and drag her by the hair—then I agree, no woman should submit. But, submission in the original sense of the word, as designed by God, has nothing to do with that.

Submitting does not mean you lose your personality and become a Stepford wife. It's not a smart way for men to have control over women. It's simply a smart way of creating partnerships in marriage. The biblical sense of this word is really about encouraging humility, gentleness, understanding, confidence in another person's leadership, flexibility, kindness and respect—the polar opposite of being defiant, rebellious, stubborn and resistant. This means that a wife needs certain qualities to work in partnership with her husband, whom she respects as a leader. Did you notice that the verse above says the wife "should" submit and let her husband lead? Notice how much power we possess! We are so strong that God feels He has to tell us that we should submit… we don't have to but we should. Yes, we should. Otherwise, we end up taking charge... But He wants us to use our strength differently, in a wiser way.

First of all, we need to understand that being submissive does not mean we are inferior to our husbands. It's simply a role that you need to fulfil so that the partnership known as marriage will function properly. Wherever two or more people plan to work together for a common goal, someone has to lead and someone has to follow. Every country has a leader, every sports team has a coach, every company has a boss and every school has a principal (headmaster). In all these examples, the concepts of leadership and submission, leader and follower, work together. This never means that the leader is a better person than the one who submits to leadership. They are simply fulfilling two different, complementary roles.

By the way, no matter what's happening with your marriage, as a woman, you already submit to various authorities and leaders—many of whom you do not know and probably do not even like. But you have to submit for the proper functioning of society or the group you belong to. This is the practical side of being submissive. It's essential to every group or society with common goals. Now, take a look at how strange this is: We're encouraged to submit to leaders we don't even know, but to rebel against the husbands who love us! Let's be smart. Submission is a smart way of dealing with the partnership known as marriage.

But you might ask, "Why do I have to submit to him, and not he to me?" Let's be honest ladies: Would you feel a sense of accomplishment after taking the lead from your husband and forcing him to take a back seat in the marriage? You'd no longer have a man by your side. No woman likes a man who doesn't take the initiative—who waits to be ordered around and given instructions—a man who's indecisive. The truth is women despise and are turned off by men like that.

Believe me when I say, we don't need to lead. We have another strength, which is the power of influence. With this, we can get whatever we want from our husbands. The power of influence is nothing more than intelligent submission. Remember, a husband is already "sold" on his wife. He wants to please her. The husband may be the head, but his wife is the neck. If she's wise, she can turn the head whichever way she wants... This is so powerful, it's scary. We have to be careful with this power so as not to destroy our husbands and ourselves.

One thing we heard the most in our Houston counselling sessions was this type of frustration: "My husband never takes the lead. I'm left to resolve everything at home. I can't take it anymore!" Little did they know that often it was their own fault...

When a woman does not submit to her husband, she ends up unintentionally castrating him. Though she doesn't mean to, she makes him out to be a nobody. Without respect, a man loses his masculinity. When you do not give him this role in the marriage, he does not feel respected and fails to fulfil his role as the man of the house.

A TRUE LEADER

The flip side of this subject is that when the Bible addressed the subject of a wife's submission, it assumed a husband's good leadership. Women were not obliged to submit to leaders who mistreated them, but rather to leaders who sacrificed and gave themselves to them. A leader treats a woman as an extension of himself—a leader in the spirit of the Lord Jesus. A true leader wants the best for his followers. Therefore, when he leads, he tries to do what is best for those under his leadership. A wise husband who wants his wife to be submissive should lead in this fashion. He should gain the respect of his follower.

A true leader is not a dictator. He seeks out and listens to the opinions and needs of his followers. His decisions benefit everyone, not just himself. This is why his leadership engenders respect, and does not need to be forced on others. A leader creates harmony: He seeks the best for his team, and in turn, they believe in his leadership and gladly submit without resistance. This is how God designed it to be: Man and woman, head and body in perfect harmony.

However, please note: Women, to a much greater degree, hold the power to create this harmony in marriage. God says she "should" submit to her husband. The power is in her hands and if she knows how to use this power, she will not lack a thing. What few people understand is that those who are genuinely submissive rarely have to submit. Because I am submissive to Renato, we rarely ever do things his way. A wife who submits to her husband can get whatever she wants from him. He is so grateful for the respect she gives him that he wants to please her, and so he ends up doing what she wants. Women, if your head's spinning because what you're reading sounds so different from anything you've ever heard—take a deep breath, stop and reread this section. This is one of the simplest yet most ignored truths in the history of humanity!

Make no mistake. Just as it's a sacrifice for men to show their feelings to their wives, it's a sacrifice for women to let their husbands lead them. It goes against her nature, and this is where many end up losing in their love lives. They're obsessed about not "losing" in the relationship, when in fact the women who submit to their husbands actually win.

And before I close:

Husbands, if you're bad leaders, if you don't make your wives feel secure, if you're selfish when it comes to decisions and careless in your behaviour (e.g. addictions), if you neglect their needs or fail to throw all your strength into caring for them—how do you expect them to submit? A wife's submission ceases to exist when her husband starts to act in a way that will hurt her. If he insists on being a bad leader and wants to walk straight off a cliff, she cannot be expected to follow him. She's going to let him walk off that cliff all by himself.

And so, when a husband satisfies the basic needs of his wife—makes her feel appreciated, loved, and safe at his side—then submission will be a very natural thing for her... even though at times she may have to hold herself back and let him lead. Now we're ready to understand and explore the basic need of men: Respect.

MEN WANT MEAT AND POTATOES

In my journey through the land of couples counselling, I've seen almost everything (I say "almost" because there's always someone who surprises us with a behaviour we've never seen before). But when it comes to men, in particular, I've come to the conclusion that we are uncomplicated and easy to please. I have seen men put up with various things from their wives without complaint: A lack of intimacy, having to eat out every day because she doesn't want to cook, babysitting while she goes out with friends, going into debt after she spends all the savings, bouts of PMS, and enduring Celine Dion concerts. Some men are true heroes. But there's one thing that I have not seen: A man who puts up with the disrespect of his wife.

Take away everything from a man, but don't take away his respect. It's the meat and potatoes of his relationship. As I think about it, men don't ask for much. But many have not even received that from their wives. And you already know what happens when a basic need is not met. That person falls back on his basic animal instincts and switches into survival mode.

When a husband isn't given the respect he deserves inside his own home, he will look for it elsewhere… and there are two main ways for a man to fill this void: A fulfilling job or another woman.

Success at work satisfies a man's need for respect. People admire and appreciate him, he's in demand, and all this makes him feel valued. So what does he do? He dives deeper into his work in an attempt to get more respect. If a woman comes along, a common event in the lives of successful men, and appreciates him in ways that his wife does not, we arrive at the formula of "how to end a marriage".

Because of this, a wise wife will not argue or be reluctant to satisfy this basic need of her husband. She simply satisfies it. And this is how she does it. Take a look:

She talks up his strength—When a wife sees her husband as strong, she's showing him respect. Unfortunately, many have swallowed the Hollywood agenda and helped destroy their husband's image of himself. They criticise him for not being "sensitive", embarrass him in public, belittle him and make no secret of it. There are women who make nasty comments and jokes about their husbands in the presence of others, and embarrass them in front of their children. Many children no longer respect their fathers because their mothers don't. Unknowingly, many women have robbed their men of their strength.

He sees himself as weak and doesn't initiate bold moves because his wife continually reminds him of his incompetence. These wives are shooting themselves in the foot. Once his confidence is destroyed, he becomes a failure. Words offend and sadden men to the point that they feel defeated and powerless. How can a man be reassuring to his wife when all this is going on?

A wise woman makes her husband feel like a hero, as if he could conquer the world. She lifts him up in word and attitude and praises his strengths both inside and outside the home. In this way she prepares him for the world and together they reap the benefits of his achievements.

She lets him be the head—She practises the concept of intelligent submission, which we explained earlier. During the few arguments they have, in which they can't reach an agreement, she lets him have the last word (of course, nothing that would be harmful to her). A wife should respect her husband's right to say "yes" or "no". Even when she knows, or thinks she knows, what his answer will be, she should consult him before doing anything. This way she reinforces the idea that his decision is valuable and important to her.

A common problem found in many of today's marriages is "the unimportant husband", who decides he's no longer going to play the marriage game. Since she doesn't respect anything he says, he stops offering his opinion and being a leader. Whether or not he agrees with an issue, she never listens. When she wants to do something, she doesn't care what he thinks. Because of this, he takes the following stance: "Go ahead. Do whatever you want. Clearly, what I think doesn't matter. Whether I agree or disagree, you're going to do it anyway, so go ahead." Hurt and reluctant, he relinquishes the decision-making to her. His wife may think she's having the upper hand, but in fact she's emasculated her husband. Ironically, these are the women who constantly complain about their husbands having no initiative and never participating in anything. Women, please understand: Men don't want to be a part of something they know they're going to lose. They will simply stop participating.

A wise woman can virtually get anything out of her husband. All she has to do is let him think it was his idea... Cristiane has become an expert at this! The secret is to bring the matter up to him, give him all the necessary information to make a decision, and then let him decide. If by chance, his decision is not what you wanted, go along with it anyway. The seed has been planted. In the near future, his natural inclination to please a woman will drive him to do something for you about that matter.

She is his number one fan—She admires her husband in spite of his faults. She's a true fan. One characteristic of a true fan is that she will keep rooting for her man even when he's losing. It's like your favourite sports team. They can lose ten games in a row, be the laughing stock of the sports world and be in last place—but you still cheer them on in the hope that they'll win one day. This is what it means to be a fan.

Every man needs to feel admired because achievements are very important to him. But like every other man, he has flaws. A wise wife will not continuously criticise or point the finger at his flaws. Instead, she will search for things to admire about him. Her admiration works on his subconscious thoughts and eventually steers him to be the man she always wanted him to be. She praises his positive qualities and pretends not to notice the negative ones. There's nothing more demoralising to a man than for his wife to be his main critic.

Acknowledge him in front of others—It's natural for women to talk about what's stressing them out, confiding in friends, mothers or any other person. But here is the danger: You expose your husband's flaws to others. Why not be an ambassador for your husband? Build up his reputation and strengthen the respect you have for him.

Make yourself attractive—Being physically attracted to his wife is a basic need for a man. Men are much more visual than women, therefore women should take care of their appearance. It puzzles me why many women are much more careful about this before marriage than after. They probably think they've now captured their man, so they no longer have to try so hard. But if he likes her with a little make-up, she should put it on out of love and keep the chemistry going. At times, because a husband knows how sensitive his wife can be, he doesn't ask her to do any of this. But she should be well aware of his needs. A wife should take care of herself to keep the flame alive. But, she should do this for her husband, not for other women, as very often happens. Find out what your husband likes. Some women want to be as thin as twigs because that's what society tells them to do, but their husbands may not like them so skinny. If magazines say that everyone's erasing their wrinkles (and facial expressions) with Botox, she blindly follows. But when her husband mentions how he'd love to see her in red lipstick, she quickly says she doesn't like that.

What is all-important for women's magazines and their readers is not always important for a woman's husband. A classic example of this is cellulite. Women panic over a hint of cellulite, but most men don't even know what that is!

Cristiane:

As women, we should not try to compete with the photoshopped models in magazines. Instead, we should invest in our femininity, which is guaranteed to grab our husband's attention. Femininity is an important part of a woman's beauty, even though fashion has stopped paying attention to it.

Years ago, I used to complain about my nose because it wasn't a perfect, upturned nose like those I saw on magazine models. I even looked into getting it "fixed". But the thought came when it was already too late. I was married. Renato would not let me get it done, and over time, he taught me to like my nose. Then I realised that I had wanted to change my nose because of what society had been telling me, not because I needed to. Renato has always said my nose was one of my facial features that caught his eye the most!

Sometimes we want to make ourselves prettier for the wrong reasons and end up ignoring what really matters to our husbands. A few years ago I found out that what Renato finds most sexy about me is my confidence, which was not always high. This means that when I was trying to find myself and kept changing my hair, the style of my clothes and my make-up, I was not sexy to him! My insecurities and attempts to change had not benefitted my marriage in any way.

A confident woman is an interesting catch for a man. After all, men are hunters. What if you were hunting in a forest, all decked out in camouflage, rifle at the ready, carefully moving closer to your prey... Suddenly, the deer notices you. But instead of running away, it trots up to you and says: "Shoot me with your rifle. Kill me. Take me home!" Without a doubt, you'd lose all interest! The intrigue of hunting comes down to the difficulty of the chase.

In the same way, a woman's mystery is what captivates her husband. Her confidence motivates him to pursue her. Women, I said confidence—not making yourself unreachable or impossible to please.

She gives him space—Men need space, time to relax and deal with their stress. This is the 'nothing box' that we've already mentioned. Many wives don't even allow their husbands time to breathe. The poor guy hardly walked through the front door and she's already piling all the stress of their day on top of him. A wise wife chooses the right time to talk, chooses what to say and how to say it. This is so important for a man. He notices the respect and confidence she has, and appreciates the fact that she doesn't feel the need to keep bugging him about the same things all the time—she immediately becomes much more attractive to him.

Of course space has its limits. A husband who always wants space and never finds the time to talk to his wife is settling on a slow death for his marriage. Insecurity and frustration will grow in her and soon she won't be able to be the wife he needs and wants. Men, space is one thing, laziness is another. There is life outside the box!

BUT HE DOESN'T DESERVE IT

Remember, all we've explained so far in this chapter is about satisfying the basic needs of men, which is for a wife to give him respect. But you may be thinking that your husband doesn't deserve your respect because of all the negative things he does. However, remember one thing:

The best thing you can do about a person's basic needs is meet them.

The truth is that no one "deserves" anything. Women may say that their husbands don't deserve their respect and men may say that their wives don't deserve their attention, but in the end if you're still together and want a bulletproof marriage, you have to take care of each other. Don't just stand there waiting for him or her to deserve it. *Do what you have to do* and in the end you'll see that your partner was worth all the effort.

Wives: Respect your husband because this is the only way to get anything out of him.

Husbands: Make your wife feel valued and cared for and you'll reap the fruit of this effort all the days of your life.

WHEN HIS BASIC NEEDS ARE HERS AND VICE-VERSA

After one of our courses in Houston where we explained the basic needs of men and women, a wife asked: "I think I'm the man in this relationship. What you said I need, he's the one who wants it, and the one thing I'm always asking him to give me is respect. What should I do?" She was a police woman. She was used to being tough and un-emotional, and married a husband who liked... attention.

In recent times, this scenario has become more common. This is not difficult to understand with women's lib and the effeminate tendencies of some men in the last few decades. We've noticed that when a man is very emotional, his wife tends to compensate by being more rational because two emotional people aren't going to get very far. But it's only a matter of time before she starts to complain because even independent women like a strong man by their side.

This new situation creates confusion for some couples. An emotional husband wants respect but isn't doing what he should do to earn it, and a rational wife wants security but finds she is unable to trust her husband...

If you find yourselves in a similar situation, here's what you should do:

- Emotional husbands, you have to overcome your insecurities in order to make your wife happy. Be less emotional and more rational. Be reassuring and mature around your wife.
- If you're an independent, rational, even bossy wife, you need to be more balanced. Allow your husband to make decisions in the relationship. Invite him to make decisions with you. Let him have the last word.

If each of you takes on the correct roles, you'll be able to walk together for the rest of your life.

> Cristiane:
>
> I'm pickier about details when compared to Renato and think about things that he forgets. On the other hand, he's more rational, gives things a lot more thought and is less impulsive. He's strong. When we're in difficult situations and I want to cry and hide in a corner, he comes with his strength, hugs me and makes me feel protected.
>
> A wise wife recognises her husband's attributes and vice-versa.

I would never have imagined the chapter on men's basic needs would turn out to be longer than the women's chapter... Why is that? It is because of your strength, woman. It takes more words to convince you... Use this strength wisely.

TASK

FOR WIVES:

Which of your husband's basic needs do you need to be more dedicated to satisfying? What are you going to do from now on to make sure he feels respected?

FOR HUSBANDS:

How can you help your wife understand your needs, without being demanding or imposing?

/BulletproofMarriage

Women, post: Now I understand my husband and what he really needs. #Bulletproofmarriage

@BulletproofMate

Women, tweet: Now I understand my husband and what he really needs. @BulletproofMate #BulletproofMarriage

/BulletproofMarriage

Men, post: I'm helping my wife understand what I need from her the most. #Bulletproofmarriage

@BulletproofMate

Men, tweet: I'm helping my wife understand what I need from her the most.

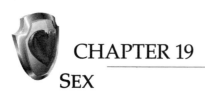

CHAPTER 19
SEX

First of all, I want to welcome all the men who want to bulletproof their marriages. This is probably the first chapter you are actually interested in reading. And to the sexually frustrated women: A light has just appeared at the end of the tunnel. There's a reason why this chapter is almost at the end of this book. Putting everything you learned in the previous chapters into practice is what will contribute to a great sex life. If you ignore everything that was said up till now, this chapter will only partially help you. So if you've skipped over chapters to get to this one more quickly, go back and read them over first. I guarantee it'll be worth it!

A healthy sex life is one of the main tools in a bulletproof marriage. It never hurts to remind people of this. The quickest way to assess the health of a relationship is to find out how they're doing in bed. If my wife and I could ask a couple only one question during a counselling session to find out how they're doing, it would be: "How's your sex life?"

Sex in a marriage is like glue that holds the couple together. It's the mystery that makes two into one. Sex says a lot. It expresses feelings and thoughts that words cannot express. When you don't seek to be physically intimate with your partner, your attitude tells them things in their head like, "You don't satisfy your husband/wife. Why is he/she ignoring me? Does he/she have someone else? There must be something wrong with me. He/she must not want me around anymore." On the other hand, when a couple has a healthy and active sex life, the unspoken messages are: "My husband finds me attractive. My wife is happy with me. We satisfy each other. There's no reason for my husband/wife to look at anyone else." The consequences of these mental messages can build up or destroy a marriage. Ignore this at your own risk.

Not only does sex speak, it cures many problems in a relationship. It is scientifically proven that intimacy has a cleansing effect—it is a mental and physical detox. And so we can safely conclude, the less you do it, the more distant you will feel, and the more problems you will have. In a sexless marriage, any small problem will be multiplied by a thousand. On the other hand, it's rare for a couple to have a bad morning after a great night in bed... Little things are brushed off because both have good credit emotionally—where sex is the strongest currency.

You can easily guess whether or not a couple is doing well sexually by observing their moods. Irritation, indifference and lack of caring are sure signs that a couple's bed is only being used for sleep. This is how powerful sex is.

The message is: Be intimate, do it well and do it regularly. But for many couples this is easier said than done. Let's unravel this mystery.

WHERE IT BEGINS AND ENDS

Counter to what many may think, sex is not what happens when a husband and wife undress and sleep together. To better understand this, think of a sandwich. When you want a sandwich, the first thing you think of is what kind you want... chicken, beef, turkey, etc. But that's not all that goes into a sandwich. You also decide on the type of bread, whether you want cheese, onion, lettuce, tomato, mustard, pickle... all those things that complement and enhance the flavour of the meat in your sandwich. You could just eat the meat by itself, but everything else makes it taste so much better.

The same goes for sex. Clearly, it is two bodies engaged in a physical act, but the act itself is simply the protein in the sandwich. It comes in the middle, but what happens before and after that act are the true beginning and end of what we call great sex. The before and after involve the mind. Yes, sex begins and ends in the mind. The physical act is the vehicle of expression, but the mind is the driver and the destination, all at the same time. Women usually do this better than men. For them, sex is connected to everything else. Remember the wires in the female brain? She can be aroused by things that would never arouse a man, simply because she associates everything with everything else. And so husbands, don't be surprised when you take the initiative at home and take out the rubbish, for example, only to have your wife looking at you as if she wants to take you straight into the bedroom when you come back in. Don't try to understand, just enjoy it!

For men, on the other hand, sex is very straightforward. All he needs to get in the mood is for her to be present. It's as if men simply have an on and off button when it comes to sex. Women on the other hand are like the cockpit of the new Boeing 787, buttons all over the place, and men don't know where to start. If he presses the wrong button, fasten your seat belt and put on your oxygen mask!

So here is a special hint for men:

Sex starts above the neck.

Men often come and ask us for advice and say something like: "My wife's never in the mood... She always has an excuse... It's like I enjoy sex and she doesn't... I don't want her to feel like she's doing me a favour... Once a month seems great for her, and sometimes that's even too much..."

Listen: Sex is very, very different for women compared to men. The mistake many husbands make is to assume that women look at sex the way they do—physical pleasure, relieving tension. Let's use another food analogy (we're all going to get hungry in a little bit). Women see sex as the cherry on top of the intimacy cake. It's an expression of the intimacy, friendship and love between you—not just in bed, but throughout the day.

Have you ever eaten the cherry without the cake? It's sweet and tasty but you're left wanting more. It doesn't satisfy your hunger, it's extremely sweet and you need something to balance it out. Well, this is how women see sex that's not preceded by intimacy. Sweet but meaningless. It won't be something she looks forward to doing again. But when the cherry is on top of a cake, it's a whole other story. The cake offers substance and the cherry enhances the flavour—a great combination.

The cake is the intimacy that precedes the bedroom. When a woman hears "intimacy" what comes to mind is a deep conversation, while men will think about putting their hands certain places. She wonders what her husband is thinking about, especially if it's about her. She loves his attention being on her and what she says. This is what strengthens a couple's intimacy.

If you've only been giving your wife cherries, now you can understand her reaction. Be a better lover to your wife by becoming a better listener and conversationalist. Dedicate more time to the cake. Connect with her.

I'm not asking you to be slick, flattering her to get what you want. Soon enough she'll notice that you are being fake and then you won't get even a cherry... I'm talking about having a sincere interest in the person who is inside your wife's body.

If you grasp this concept, that for women sex begins above the neck, both of you will be much happier in bed and everywhere else, and there won't be enough cake for so many cherries...

I DON'T LIKE SEX

This is almost as ridiculous as saying "I don't like air", the only difference is that nobody dies from a lack of sex. But saying you don't like sex is not reasonable unless there is something physically wrong with you. Sex is a healthy thing and extremely pleasurable. God created it... and God doesn't make bad things. If people say they don't like sex it is because they don't know what it is, or they know but their partners don't. So if a husband likes sex and his wife doesn't, it's his responsibility to help her find out how good it can be for her. I say "for her" because the goal of intimacy is to satisfy your partner. Many women don't care to have sex because they feel their husbands use them for their own personal pleasure.

I want to make something clear: It's a husband's obligation to make sure his wife has an orgasm. The goal of sex is to please your partner, not to please yourself. Because of selfish attitudes like this many end up saying "I don't like sex". Everyone enjoys sex when it's done the way God intended—to completely satisfy your partner.

But for this to happen, both have to regard each other's pleasure as their top priority. The obvious, logical way of doing this would be to put a woman's pleasure first, then a man's. Women usually take longer than men, so if men think of themselves first, women will be left out in the cold.

To sum things up, sex is both a necessity and a pleasure, and it's an activity that strengthens and protects a marriage. What are some tips for a great sex life? We have five for you.

FIVE INGREDIENTS FOR A GREAT SEX LIFE

1. Clear your mind—First, clear your mind of any and all dirty thoughts about sex. You may have to decontaminate your mind from all the warped information that you've accumulated from friends, magazines, pornography and so forth. There's an abundance of filth, distortion and misinformation about this subject. Understand one thing: When God created man and woman, they didn't need pornography or a manual to have sex. He designed sex for a couple's pleasure and enabled them to satisfy each other without the intervention of others. You and your partner are all you need to achieve great intimacy. So don't view sex as dirty or taboo. It is God's gift to you. It is one of the few things in life that is exclusive to both of you. Friendships are not exclusive to marriage. Sharing material possessions is not exclusive to marriage, neither is being faithful (you can be faithful to your job). But sex is exclusive to a couple. So treat it with the importance, purity and value it deserves.

2. Use your mind to connect—Remember, sex is connected to everything that precedes the actual act, especially for women. Sex begins and ends in the mind. Take time to admire your spouse with your mind. This is a conscious, voluntary decision you have to make, or else other concerns that have nothing to do with your partner will enter your thoughts. Stress is the biggest factor for low sexual drive and impotence. You need to set aside time to mentally connect with your partner, no matter how busy or stressed you might be at your job or with other issues. Turn yourself off to whatever might try to divert your attention away from your spouse. Comment on each other's clothes, her beauty, his handsomeness, the parts of each other's bodies that you like the most, ask her what she's thinking about, her plans and projects, her concerns— listen carefully and offer help, encouragement and security. Women should not expect men to be as open about their thoughts as girls are because men do not need to do this to feel "connected". But women should sprinkle their day with kind remarks, unexpected physical contact, a sexy look, a compliment about one of their manly traits—how strong he is, his determination or intelligence. All these things are pre-sex.

3. Focus on your partner—The pleasure you get from satisfying your partner should be as great as your own pleasure. In fact, this is one of the main secrets to making your husband or wife crazy about you. Your focus should be on your partner, not on yourself! If she reaches climax, yours will be the result of that. Think about what is important to the other person. A crucial point that normally differs between men and women is privacy. He might not consider it much of a problem if someone in the next room hears moans and groans. It adds to his manhood. On the other hand, if she doesn't have a heart attack first, she'll never be able to look that other person in the eye. Let's not even mention one of your children wandering into the room wanting to know what all the noise is about. So men, focus on what's important to her. Women need to feel safe and private before they can loosen up. Lock the bedroom door. Soundproof your bedroom walls if necessary. Respect her and be discreet. In fact, women need to feel secure, not only when it comes to privacy but with your behaviour as well. If you lie to her, hide information, are irresponsible with money, and have an unpredictable temper, she will not feel comfortable or safe with you. Didn't we warn you that women connect sex to everything else? Now a tip for the women: If your husband tries really hard to make you reach the clouds, then right after, make him reach the stars. It's your turn to focus on him...

4. Discover and explore each other—Nobody is the same. What one woman thinks is amazing, another woman may hate. This is why you should be each other's lovers and find out what excites your partner. What parts of her body does she like you to touch? What does she not like to be touched? Ask your wife, explore her likes and dislikes rather than consult websites and magazines for this information. These things are very personal. Some men like (or have read that women like) something that causes their wives to feel uncomfortable during sex. You commonly find things like "7 ways to drive your man crazy in bed" on magazine covers. Things like this sell because people are very ignorant about the subject, and so they read this stuff. Be extremely careful with what you bring into your mind and bedroom. Not everything that's in magazines (actually, almost nothing) is good for you. Sexual pleasure comes from exploring the person you're married to. I don't care if a magazine says that women like this or that. What if my wife doesn't like it? Not all women are the same. They aren't robots, nor were they created as a series. Couples need to have a dialogue, have conversations, find out what each other enjoys, and adapt to one another. It is also important to find out how frequently your spouse would like to be intimate. For example, having sex once a week might be enough for her. On the other hand, her husband wants to have sex every day. In this case, they need to agree on a middle ground. She'll have to be a bit more understanding and agree to be sexually intimate at least three times a week, and he'll have to sacrifice and be happy with only three times a week... or twice... or four times. What is important is that you adapt to each other. Never impose something on your spouse, especially sex. When it's forced and not natural, it will be very unpleasant. When something is not good for one partner, it's not good for either person. Respect each other's boundaries. For example, if you like oral sex and your partner doesn't, don't force the situation.

5. Invest in foreplay—When was the last time you gave each other a passionate kiss... or gave your partner a lengthy massage? Have you caressed your wife lately? Have you run your fingers through her hair, touched her neck and ended with a hug? The romance that unfolds during the day and the hours before intimacy comes to a climax when both actually engage in the act. This moment requires a great deal of self-control from men. Studies show that on average men ejaculate two to three minutes after penetration. On the other hand, women need an average of seven to 12 minutes to reach orgasm. Can you see where the problem lies? Men need to climb the mountain slowly being careful not to reach the top just as their wives are putting on their boots... This is when a smart man, who's been practising all the steps we've explained so far in this book, has an advantage. A woman who's been romanced over the last 24 hours will not need as much warming up before the actual act. However, men still need to control themselves and keep at their wives' pace instead of rushing ahead. Women can help their husbands by maintaining a more active sex life. If he has sex with you once a month or less, it'll be difficult for him to control himself when you're together.

WAIT, IT'S NOT OVER YET!

We said that sex begins and ends in the mind, and the actual act in itself is just the filling of the sandwich. This means that after both have reached orgasm (yes, this is the goal) intimacy itself is still not over. Of course, at this point, both are physically satisfied, and a man in particular might feel like rolling over and going to sleep—but not men who've read Bulletproof Marriage! They know that the moments immediately after sex are when their wives are feeling closer and more connected with them than ever. And so, this is when he needs to maintain the physical contact, show affection, say sweet things and pay compliments. You cannot under any circumstances allow your wife to feel used. Understand that this is the best time to make her feel loved and—honestly—to begin to prepare her for the next time!

THE MOTHER-IN-LAW I ASKED GOD FOR

Cristiane:

Shortly before I got married, still very young and inexperienced, my mother taught me something about sex that I've always kept in mind: "You won't always feel like making love with your husband, but don't go by what you feel. Do it anyway. Once you start, you'll end up enjoying it. Never say 'no' to him, so that he never feels rejected."

Up to this very day, Renato thanks her for this advice!

Both men and women like sex. I don't believe the myth that says women like it less than men. The problem is many men don't know how women view it. For her, sex is the climax of a day filled with love: Dialogue, caresses, caring, glances, patience and everything else that is good and triggered by the love her husband showed her throughout the day. When a husband puts this into practice, his wife will probably end up wanting to have sex more often than him...

However, the truth is you won't be showered with romance every single day. There will be bad days and normal days. Don't expect every night or every intimate moment to be marked by fire and passion. That just doesn't happen. Don't live in a fantasy world. There are times when you'll have to begin the act when you're not really in the mood. At times your partner will want to be intimate and you won't feel like it. But when this happens, just decide to get in the mood. Don't be lazy. Go ahead, participate. Never reject your partner. Remember, sex talks. One unreasonable rejection can create little monsters inside your spouse's head. This is why couples should make love even when they're tired. With the busy lifestyles we have today, who isn't tired at the end of the day? One thing is certain: The more you do it, the more you'll want to do it; the less you do it, the less you'll want to do it.

This is such a serious matter that the Bible itself says[18] you don't have the right to deny your husband or wife when they want to be sexually intimate. Women are not meant to be their husband's sex slave. The explanation given in the Bible is much more beautiful and profound: Your body is not yours, it's his, and his body is not his, it's yours. You belong to one another. If one denies pleasure to the other, he will be

---

[18] Corinthians 7:3-5

breaking the covenant of marriage, and giving room for the devil to act. (How many people are opening the doors of their marriage to the devil because of this?)

When one of you is sexually frustrated because the other is always unavailable, adultery may sneak in—a major cause of broken marriages. Obviously, if the reason you are holding back has to do with pain or some other physical difficulty, you need to speak to one another and seek medical help.

PHASES AND STAGES

A warning sign along the road of a couple's sexuality: Stay tuned to the phases and stages of your marriage and life. Certain events, factors and changes will inevitably affect your intimacy. This doesn't necessarily mean things will get worse, but you have to adapt and be more understanding of each other. Something you will have to bear in mind is that sex at 50 is not the same as in your 20s. Another thing to bear in mind is any large difference in age—for example, he is 45 and she is 35.

After a pregnancy, women tend to be less interested in sex. Husbands need to understand that the arrival of a child changes everything in a marriage. His wife will be tired from taking care of the baby (if you don't think so, try taking care of a baby for 24 hours and see for yourself), her body will have changed and she will be sleep deprived. Husbands have to understand and reduce their expectations in this department. His wife, however, should not use this as an excuse. Her sexual desire may have decreased, but his is still the same... The baby needs you, but also a father. Do not neglect your husband.

When a man is going through tough times at work, his sexual drive also tends to decrease. Failure at work may be demoralising to a man and can even cause impotence. Wives should wisely support their husbands and make them feel "manly" by constantly admiring, supporting and encouraging them.

Different work schedules (that keep the couple apart), long trips and health issues are other factors that can affect a couple's sexual activity. My advice is that you remain alert to these signs and make the necessary changes so that they do not affect you negatively.

CAN WE DO THAT?

Few subjects raise more doubt and questions than sex. We're constantly asked if this or that can be done during sex. Instead of answering all these questions in detail, I want to point out something important for all couples, a general guide.

The most sexually frustrated couples worry the most about this subject. They are usually women who are overly worried about the sexy lingerie they're going to wear (for most men, any kind of lingerie is sexy), visit sex shops, worry about what this or that magazine says about sex, are extremely concerned about weight gain and having their husbands notice them. Or they could be men who've developed an addiction to pornography and masturbation, and who've stopped being their wives' real life lovers to fantasise about women they will never meet.

Remember: Don't base your life on people who have a bad marriage. Celebrities and "relationship experts" who are glamourised by the media are commonly unhappy in love. Married for the third or fourth time, divorced, cheating and being cheated on, or never able to find true love. If there is anyone who you should not want to receive love life advice from, it would be these people. And so, don't let the confusion of this world complicate what God made simple.

Follow these common-sense rules: Be your husband or wife's lover. Explore and discover one another. Don't impose or demand that your partner do anything they do not want to do. Do not do anything that goes against nature (anal sex). Focus on pleasing your partner and do not be selfish. The rest, you will develop on your own.

If you want to check out our answers on several other specific questions about sex, visit our website at www.bulletproofmarriage. org/sex

 ## TASK:

Need I spell it out what you should do now?

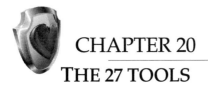

CHAPTER 20
THE 27 TOOLS

Over the course of our marriage and after years of counselling couples with a wide variety of marital problems, Cristiane and I have developed what we call "tools" to deal with all sorts of situations that might arise. Some of these we created for ourselves, and others we learned or acquired from other wise couples. We've selected the best, and written them in this chapter for you to have at your disposal.

Every household should have a toolbox. You need one when you want to hang pictures, fix a wobbly drawer, or unclog a drain. Every marriage needs specific tools as well. The 27 listed here will help you repair and maintain your marriage. Most likely they won't all apply to the situations you're in right now, but this information will help you assemble your own toolbox to use in marriage emergencies. Like any other toolbox, you don't need all of the items to do one job, but it's always good to have them handy, because you never know when they might be needed.

Most of these are tools that you probably already know, but aren't putting into practice. Their strength lies in using them in tandem with other tools, which may be why you haven't seen results when you only used one tool on its own. Also, you didn't know then what you know now, from reading this book. So rally your strength and apply them again, but this time combine them as needed. Open up your toolbox and start adding the following tools inside, one by one—and learn how to apply them in the right situations.

1. Don't sleep on it—Don't go to bed with an unresolved issue between you. Make it a point not to allow problems to fester by telling yourself you'll deal with them later. The Scriptures say, *Be angry and do not sin: Do not let the sun go down on your wrath, nor give place to the devil*[19]. In other words, it's not a sin to be angry, but it is a sin to let your anger linger into the following day, often causing you to do something irrational because of it. They say that time heals all wounds, but this is hardly true. An open wound only gets worse with time.

Problems start off like little green baby monsters—fragile, small, and seemingly harmless. They feed off of silence and indifference, and grow while you sleep. If no one does anything about them, you end up with giant green monsters as pets that chew you up and tear you both apart. The sooner you kill them (preferably, while they're still unhatched), the less the damage they cause. It's easy to know whether or not you've killed your monster. If you're sleeping with your backs to each other or in separate rooms, it means that the issue hasn't been resolved yet, and the monster is still terrorising your marriage. Talk it over again and reconcile with your partner.

This tool was something that Cristiane and I developed to solve our problem of the silent treatment. We agreed: "From now on, whenever we have a problem, let's stay up and talk about it until it's resolved." Of course this resulted in many nights of going to bed at three in the morning, but eventually we'd fall asleep in each other's arms. We'd wake up happy the next day, because we wouldn't drag any negativity from the previous day into the new day. When we were strict about using this

---

[19] Ephesians 4:26,27

tool, the silent treatments ended. I learned how to solve a problem once and for all. A problem stuck on the back burner is a problem that only worsens.

Many couples go through this. Your spouse wants to resolve an issue, but you don't because you think it's already been resolved, or because you're upset and don't want to deal with it. Ignore your emotions and do what's right. Using the 10 steps to problem solving, explained in Chapter 6, will help you with this.

The words *"nor give place to the devil"* in the verse above reveal a lot. When you have unresolved issues that make you angry, you are giving place to the devil. During any particular time in your relationship, you're either in the presence of God or in the presence of the devil. Please understand this. You should develop a sensitivity to distinguish when you're in the presence of one or of the other. Watch for the signs, they're easy to see. When God is present, your relationship goes well. When the devil is present, things are a tangled mess. This means that he found a gap to squeeze into your relationship. So hurry up and close that gap, now!

Use this tool: If something is unresolved or left "up in the air"; when you're holding something against your partner; when one is giving the other the cold shoulder.

2. Love never hurts—There's no excuse for hurting your partner physically, verbally, emotionally, or any other way. Being angry is not an excuse for hurting the other person. True love never hurts. How many times do we get angry about something that happens at work? So what do we do, beat up our boss? Kick the chairs? Don't we learn how to manage our anger without hurting others around us? You know that if you attack your boss (or anyone else in the company), you'll lose your job, so you learn how to manage your anger to avoid any inappropriate behaviour with co-workers. Do the same with your loved one. Never be aggressive towards them. And don't use the excuse that you're just a short-tempered person. True love does not inflict pain. This also goes for hurtful words that can erupt when a couple is having an argument. They swear at each other as though their spouse meant nothing to them, but someone who is part of our own body should never be treated this way. Don't drag yourself into the gutter by swearing at your spouse or attacking their character.

Happy couples treat each other with high standards. They refuse to accept harmful behaviour. The lower the tolerance for bad behaviour, the happier the couple will be over time. For example, when a wife swears at her husband and he retaliates, both break the rules of behaving in a civilised manner. If you don't fix the situation by apologising and promising to never act like that again, forget it! Once you cross that line, you'll cross it again, until you end up reaching a point of no return. We counsel many couples who tell us about a recent argument and then say to each other: "Sorry, but I was just being honest, that's how I feel." You don't always need to say exactly what you feel. Our emotions can make us come up with crazy thoughts. Sometimes, how you feel isn't really what you think. If you act on impulse and blurt out your feelings, you inflict wounds that your spouse may not be able to recover from.

Use this tool: When your emotions are about to get the better of you and you feel like you're about to explode. Memorise this phrase: "Love never hurts." Be civil. If your partner hurts your feelings, respectfully insist, without adding fuel to the fire, to treat each other with higher standards. You may have to talk about it later after tempers have calmed down, but don't let it get the better of you.

3. Do not generalise—However you complete these sentences, "You always…" and "You never…" it will probably land you in trouble. Don't use the brush of one situation to paint the entire character of your partner. "You always do what you like, never what I like." "You never listen to me." These sentences can hardly ever be true. They will anger your partner. Deal with the matter at hand and resist the temptation to connect it to the past. Watch out for the words "never", "always", "nothing", "everything" and "every time". These are absolute terms and leave no other options. Avoid them.

This problem is most common in women. A wife *feels* like her husband always has *that attitude*, based on so many past experiences. She expresses what she is *feeling*, which is not exactly a fact. The problem is that if a woman says, "You never take me out," her husband will automatically remember that he took her out once, two months ago. So he says, "I never...? But I took you out to see that movie..." and flips the problem back onto her. When you generalise, your spouse can usually remember a fact to disprove your statement. He then drives home his point that your complaint is invalid, he's convinced he's off the hook, and then the real issue gets side-tracked.

How do you deal with a problem if you constantly hear generalisations? Understand that she is probably not saying that you literally "never" or "always" do something. What she is expressing is how she feels about that situation. Hear: "This happens so often that I feel like you never take me out," instead of, "You never take me out." Be patient. Don't get irritated and keep the focus on the issue that she is bringing to the table and her need for you to help resolve it.

Use this tool: Whenever you have a conversation. If generalisations are used at any point during the conversation, apologise and rephrase your words. If your partner constantly generalises, pinpoint the problem, so that you don't repeat these inaccurate words in the future. Focus on what he or she is really saying and deal with it.

4. Stop nagging and start praying—Does your partner repeatedly do things that irritate you and doesn't want to change? Have you been nagging for years, and noticed that it's a useless waste of time? Then nag God. Ask Him to touch your partner's heart and give you the wisdom to deal with your situation. Of course when someone feels attacked, they're focused on defending themselves and aren't willing to see their own faults. But God can make them see. Prayer has a thousand and one uses. Besides being a tool that can bring about the changes that you can't create alone, it also helps you deal with stress as you place your anxieties in God's hands. He can handle all your frustration and anger with a problem for as long as it remains. You, on the other hand, wouldn't be able to withstand all of that. Think about it, you're turning to the One who created marriage to solve your problem. It's like complaining directly to the manufacturer, like calling customer service and speaking directly to the owner. But be persistent. Answers don't always appear overnight. Keep praying. Pray for yourself as well, so that you won't be part of the problem. Ask for wisdom to deal with the situation.

Cristiane:

When I realised that constant nagging wasn't changing my husband, I came to the conclusion that I couldn't fix that situation alone and sought help from God. This tool is a change of direction: Stop acting on emotion, and instead act on faith by trusting in God. But make no mistake, God is not a magician and He doesn't work alone. He does His part when you do your part. And if you don't know how to do your part, ask Him for guidance. Women tend to nag to the point of aggravation. We think that we can solve problems by complaining. I began praying and asking Him to change my own behaviour. I wanted to stop crying about the problem and start acting by faith, and I was only able to do that through prayer. Only God can change your spouse. Only He can change someone from the inside out. Before, I prayed that God would change Renato, but after seeking God's guidance to show me what to do, I began to seek out ways to change myself first. And that was when I began noticing a change in my husband. God not only gives us comfort and peace, but He also guides us in what to do. This principle can work in every area of our lives.

Use this tool: When all else fails.

5. Show appreciation—Married people will sometimes be drawn into an affair simply because someone else appreciates them more than their wife or husband. When you sense your partner is distant, or you yourself feel distant, you need to consciously make the effort to show your appreciation for your spouse, e.g. cook him something he likes, make dinner special, wash up and get ready for him when he comes home, be home when he comes home; check in on her, call her during the day, notice her new outfit, go out with her and do something that she likes. It's very easy to take each other for granted after a few years of marriage.

Various situations can divert a couple's focus, causing them to forget about each other over the years and slip into a phase of indifference. Once kids come along, they can consume all of a couple's energy. A woman's life can easily revolve around them and her husband gets pushed aside. If both are struggling to grow a business or to pay off debts, their needs for appreciation get sidelined. Or when the children finally leave home and get married, a couple can feel like they've become strangers, unable to relate to each other because they've lost that bond. The appreciation tool becomes very useful at these times. Identifying the phase of indifference is easy. Just take a look at the two. They are no longer a unit. Each one lives in his or her own little world. One in front of the TV, the other glued to the computer. One goes to sleep before the other. They go out alone, live separate lives and have very little in common. A couple who lives like this rarely shows each other any appreciation, because you need to notice others to appreciate them. But this can change, even after years of indifference, if you want it to. Remember the little things you did for each other while you were dating and early on in your marriage? Remember how much you cared about your spouse? That's what needs to be brought back to the relationship. I'm going to repeat a sentence that you will often find throughout this book (something you can't forget): A happy marriage takes work. Even to this day I invest in my marriage. It's a constant but rewarding job.

A question I'd like every couple to memorize is: *What does my spouse need from me right now?* If you don't know, try to find out. (They won't always tell you. Or they might say "nothing" when the truth is, they have a long list of things listed in alphabetical order.) Ask yourself: *"What can I do for him/her?"* She may be feeling stressed or upset, in need of your company or encouragement. She turns to you because she knows that she has a strong person by her side. Sometimes just one word is enough, or even simply comforting her in silence, assuring her that everything will work out, that she's just going through a phase and will overcome it. If she's sick, she needs to feel cared for, or at least know that you care about what she's going through.

Women, don't think that this job is only for men. Sometimes a man might be feeling dejected and needs to hear some encouraging words to show him that you still see him as strong. Warning: Most men do not know how to receive compliments, but it doesn't mean they don't like it. You may have already tried to encourage him and seen no real response. A wife may compliment his clothes and he simply shrugs. Don't be discouraged! Believe me, he simply doesn't want to give away his feelings... This is quite common and involuntary, almost like a manufacturer's defect. Even if he does not know how to receive a compliment, don't stop complimenting him. You may not see his inner feelings, but don't worry, it really is working.

Psychologist John Gottman, a respected relationship expert, conducted a study that led him to conclude the following: For every negative experience a couple has, five positive experiences are required to compensate for the negative one. Let's say that a couple exchanged harsh words and upset each other. If they want to make amends, they need to perform five positive actions in order to nullify that one negative experience. Gottman's theory leads us to believe that bad experiences are five times more powerful than good ones. For this reason, when a husband does something that makes his wife stop trusting him, she still clearly remembers what happened one month later. So the more you appreciate your partner, the more positive impressions you will accumulate in your relationship.

Use this tool: Always, especially when you start noticing a distance or indifference between you and your partner.

6. When your partner asks you to do something, do it first—Much of the stress in a relationship comes from the thought that we are not as important to our spouse as something or someone else. So when your partner asks you for something, put it at the top of your list. Make it a priority, so they don't need to ask you again. It's a simple rule of thumb, but it's worth its weight in gold.

A husband asks, "Honey, I'm out of razors, could you buy me some more when you go to the store?" His wife answers with a, "Yeah okay," but wasn't really paying much attention. The next day, he looks for the razors and they're not there. He gets a little upset but doesn't say anything. She apologises and promises to buy more the next time. But then the story repeats itself the next day. Is it trivial? Yes, but couples fight over trivial things. Why do they fight? Because that triviality is actually whispering something very serious in their spouse's ear like: "I don't mean anything to you," "If your mother asked you to do something, you'd drop everything, run off and do it, but when I ask, you ignore me." That's the real problem. The razors aren't the problem. The problem lies in the hidden message behind your attitude. You should incorporate this rule into your daily life. When he or she asks you for something, get it done quickly, because this will solidify the fact that you come first in each other's lives. Think about it. When your boss asks you for something, you make a habit of getting it done as soon as possible. You know that person is important because they can influence what happens to you. Well then, how much truer is this in your marriage! Your husband/ wife is far more important. Maybe your spouse has been asking you for something for quite a while and you haven't done it. It could be anything from something that seems trivial to a serious conversation that's been long overdue. Get it done right now, make it a priority, as evidence of your consideration.

Use this tool: Whenever he/she asks you for something.

7. Look after your looks—Many people who used to be really careful about their looks while they were dating, see marriage as a licence to look ugly... If anything, it's AFTER marriage that you need to look after yourself the most. Never take your partner for granted, assuming that you have already won him or her over. Purposefully seek to look beautiful for your partner. Watch your weight, how you dress, wear make-up (if your husband likes it). Cleanliness and tidiness of your home are very important too.

Some women don't like wearing make-up, but their husbands might enjoy seeing them in lipstick or eyeshadow. A woman may think that her husband has to like her for her natural beauty: *"This is the way I am."* Of course, I'm not going to like Cristiane just because of her earrings or make-up, but if a woman knows that her husband likes these things, she should make the effort to please him. Just like when it comes to food. If one of you likes to eat something that the other doesn't, then allow your spouse to enjoy the things he or she likes to eat rather than forcing your tastes on them all the time.

That's what marriage is all about, living to please the other person, to make the other person happy. Okay, I agree that it's not fair to demand that a spouse become someone they aren't, but it won't kill you to make the effort to please your spouse, and in the end you'll feel better about yourself. At work, I have to wear a suit, tie, dress shirt and dress shoes. In my leisure time, I like flip-flops, shorts and t-shirts, because I almost never get to wear them. When we first got married, going to the movies meant that I would wear sweats and flip-flops, because I wanted to be comfortable. For her, this was a special date, so she'd get all dressed up. Just picture us together! She wouldn't say anything, but she felt embarrassed by me. When she finally said: "Those clothes make you look like you gave up on life," I got upset, but later I understood. We rarely went out, so when we did, I had to honour her and rise to her level. I make an effort because I love her, and because she likes it. But for me, I'd rather just go out in flip-flops!

We counselled a couple in which the husband was sexually frustrated. He complained that whenever he sought to be intimate with his wife, she rejected him. As he spoke, we noticed that she was embarrassed. We asked to speak to them separately, so they'd feel freer to speak in private. That's when she finally opened up: *He says I never want him to touch me, but couldn't he at least take a shower every day?* She had to be superwoman to endure intimate moments with a guy who had no clue about cleaning up after work. He was so used to a lack of hygiene that he didn't even realise it was driving a wedge between them. Something that was so easy to resolve! Soap, hot water, a towel and *voilà*! The end of their problems.

237

Cristiane:

You represent your spouse, so after you get married your responsibility about your looks grows even more. Your appearance says a lot about how you feel. When you're happy and feel accomplished, it reflects outwardly. If you love, respect and value your husband, it's only natural that it shows. You could very well be unhappy on the inside and yet look good on the outside, but there is no way that you can be happy on the inside and look bad outwardly. Not only with the way you dress, but your face, your smile, a tender look. Can a woman who puts on a grumpy face when her husband gets home, be happy? Can a woman who goes out with a scowl and sloppily dressed, be happy? How does a husband feel when he looks at his wife and sees a bitter, shabby woman?

If you are feeling irritable because it's that time of the month, tell your husband. Make it very clear that the problem is hormonal (he will understand that he needs to be patient). Don't let him think he is the problem, or that you are unhappy with him. Appearance is not everything in my life, but if I love and value myself, why not take care of myself too? And I should do this even more now that I represent someone else.

Use this tool: Always. And find out what pleases your spouse regarding your appearance. Also communicate your preferences, but don't impose anything.

8. Never ridicule your partner—privately or publicly. Being funny is not the same thing as making fun of someone. Beware of distasteful jokes. Don't expose your spouse's flaws and weaknesses to others. "Love *covers* all sins," says the wisdom of King Solomon[20]. Love hides the other's flaws. Even if your partner is wrong, support them rather than

---

[20] Proverbs 10:12

expose their mistakes. Teasing is disrespectful. Don't make comments that are a putdown to your spouse or reveal something that he has not yet made public. "Robert doesn't even know how to add. He only made it to the 8th grade." How do you think this will benefit your marriage? Sarcasm, irony and disrespect are also fatal to any relationship. "You're going to write a to-do list? Since when are you any good with lists?" This attitude just shows that one spouse feels superior to other. Remember, love does not hurt.

Use this tool: Always. Be extra careful to implement this when in a heated argument or among friends.

9. Drink some Holy Water—There's a story about a village where marital strife was rife. Tired of arguing with her husband, a wife went one day to seek advice from the village's wise man. "What do I do so my husband and I won't argue anymore?" she asked. The old man handed her a bottle of water and said, "This is holy water. Every time your husband starts an argument, drink some of this water—but keep it in your mouth for ten minutes before swallowing. And tell all your neighbours to do the same." Soon nobody argued in that village any more! Remember, it takes two to argue. When your partner is angry, you should calm down. If your spouse makes a comment that causes you to want to argue back, you can decide not to participate in this argument. You don't have to ignore the problem, but you can keep your cool, especially if you decide to control your tongue. Tempers will calm down and you will avoid an unnecessary argument, which would only push you both further apart. At times, we have to concede a temporary "victory" in order to win a permanent one.

Winning an argument is not as important as solving the problem. If you notice that your partner is getting aggravated, hold back and zip your lips. I'll never forget a couple from Singapore, who attended our church meetings in London. On the day we offered a special prayer for their 50th wedding anniversary, we asked them what had been their secret to such a long-lasting life together. The husband replied: "When I get mad, she keeps quiet. When she gets mad, I keep quiet." This really does work.

Use this tool: When you feel the urge to retaliate with harsh words.

10. Initiate conversation with a soft start-up—If you begin your conversation with a harsh tone, you will inevitably end up in an argument, even if there are many attempts to restore the peace afterwards. Some classic examples: if the husband asks, "Do you need money?" (Good start) and the wife replies, "Just to pay the bills you didn't pay last week" (harsh response)—the daggers of accusation and sarcasm start to fly across the room. When the conversation starts well, chances are that it will finish well too. Choose your words carefully, do a mental test of what you are about to say and see if it sounds good. If you think that the other person may misinterpret you, rephrase it. The conversation will have slowed down and you will have had time to think and avoid stepping in a mess. If you notice that things have got out of line, take a deep breath, ask for forgiveness and start again.

> Cristiane:
> One effective way is to tell your spouse how you <u>feel</u> about the problem, instead of treating him like he is the problem. For example, if your husband is rude to you, it's not wise to call him rude, because you're starting off on an offensive note and he'll only try to defend himself. But you can tell him how you feel when he speaks like that to you… "Honey, I feel bad when you answer me this way." See the difference? He isn't the one who makes you feel bad, it's the way he answers you.

Focus on what you think and feel about the problem, instead of attacking the person involved in the problem.

Use this tool: Whenever you're dealing with a sensitive issue.

11. The filing cabinet of perpetual problems—I'm sorry to say, but there are certain flaws and things that irritate us about our partners that will never change. Perhaps he will always be messy. Maybe she'll always be a mama's girl. There are things in each of us that are part of our identity, and will not change. Instead of getting frustrated and confronting the other person about it, take this problem and put it in the filing cabinet of perpetual problems—a little place in your brain that is reserved to remind you that it's useless to continue debating about this issue. The best thing for you to do is learn to deal with it. Put more laundry baskets in strategic places around the house. And even after you've done this, pick up the items that he still throws on the floor. Accept your wife's friendship with your mother-in-law—join them! If it's a tolerable problem that you are able to handle, then use this tool.

Stop trying to change the other person, because it won't happen. As we said in the beginning: you can only change yourself. Take the focus off your partner's flaws. Appreciate your spouse's qualities and the contents in this filing cabinet will begin to have less and less importance in your relationship.

Use this tool: When you identify a perpetual problem.

12. Delete the last ten seconds—From time to time we have to let some things go. One word that is said out of line, an unnecessary comment in a time of anger... Assess the situation and see if it's really worth getting into a heated argument about it. There will be times when your wife gets under your skin and you'll want to explode, but remember:

you don't *need to* explode. When you use a video camera and don't like what you just filmed, you go back and record new images to replace the old ones. In the same way, you can use this mental tool to "stop, rewind and delete", by telling your spouse, "Okay, I'm going to pretend that I didn't see or hear what just happened. We started off on the wrong foot. Let's start over."

This tool to erase the last ten seconds happens to be my own invention. I noticed that Cristiane sometimes acted on impulse or was driven by frustration, and ended up saying things she didn't really want to say. Instead of reacting angrily, I would—in a light-hearted manner—give her the signal that she was a little out of line. If she'd say something hurtful to me, I'd say, "Wait, let me rewind the tape right here. Ok, take 2. Action!" When she hears this, she understands that what she said was not appropriate and has a chance to rephrase it. Incidentally, if you failed to use the tool of "beginning with a soft start-up", you get another chance to avoid trouble using this tool and erasing the last ten seconds. Use this tool to change the mood and the situation. Help the other person out, don't take the harsh words they're saying to heart and give them a chance to rewind and begin again.

Use this tool: When your partner steps out of line and you feel like strangling them with that line!

13. Don't let your body language cancel out your words—Communication experts say that over 90% of a conversation is non-verbal. Look at this number—more than 90%! Things like demeanour, tone of voice, eyes, facial expressions, body language are responsible for almost all of what we convey. Our words carry less than 10% of our communication with another person. Saying, "Okay, I forgive you," while your face says (as you roll your eyes), "I'm only saying this because you asked, but I know you'll never change," does not make your forgiveness appear sincere.

Besides facial and body language, something that speaks louder than your words is your recent behaviour. If you say "I'll change," yet have already promised it a hundred times and never did, your words have no credibility. So don't even think about complaining when your spouse doesn't believe you.

Pay attention to your non-verbal signals. It happens all the time in conversations. When a husband crosses his arms and says, "Okay, what do you want to say?" he's actually saying: "I'd rather be any-where else than having this conversation. But don't you dare say that I didn't stop and listen." All this can be said without even saying a word. Body language and tone of voice that are more receptive, are the secrets to good communication. Don't expect your conversation to turn out well when your demeanour is uptight and defensive, your tone is sarcastic, or you're sighing loudly. Always keep in mind that your partner is not an enemy, and your goal is to end the conversa-tion well. Being open to dialogue is a prerequisite for this to happen. Try to communicate with your spouse in a loving, enjoyable and non-threatening manner. What both of you want is a healthy rela-tionship, isn't it? You need to want it with all of your strength, and with all of your body—literally.

Use this tool: In every conversation.

14. Rebuilding trust is a two-person job—If you've experienced unfaithfulness in your relationship, whether you're the culprit or the victim, you have to work hard and work TOGETHER to rebuild trust. A common mistake is to blame only the one who was unfaithful: "It's all your fault, you're the one who gave me reason to be suspicious of you in the first place." We can easily believe that the offender is the only one who has to work to rebuild trust. But that is not the case. It takes both of you to make that happen.

This applies to any situation where trust has been broken. For example, a wife spends more than she should have, and now her husband no longer trusts her with money. In the case of unfaithfulness, the pain and suspicion will constantly haunt your thoughts, always asking, "Will it happen again?"

If you were unfaithful, you will have to do things differently to prove there has been a real change and to regain trust. Don't complain about it, just do it. It's the price of your unfaithfulness.

Cut out the covert phone calls, stop deleting text or voice messages from your cell phone, allow your partner to have the passwords to your e-mail accounts, Facebook, and any other social sites. Some things have to stop being a part of your life, such as going out without saying where you're going or who you're with, secrecy, hiding information from your partner, or refusing to answer questions about your daily activities. This behaviour will only continue to fuel distrust. For trust to be salvaged, the person who betrayed his or her partner needs to sear the word *transparency* into his or her mind. When you're transparent, you have nothing to hide, which eventually builds your reputation as trustworthy.

Be transparent in everything and don't complain about it. Don't come up with excuses like, "What about my privacy?" or "I'm not doing it anymore, you have to trust me." You gave up your privacy on your wedding day. And if your spouse is giving you another chance and has forgiven you, it's transparency that will serve as a bridge to rebuild confidence, not just promises. It's like a criminal who is taken to court. A first-time offender may be eligible for probation. The judge will impose a few restrictions: Stay within the county line, report to your probation officer on a weekly basis, etc.—but all is offered in exchange for not going to prison. If a criminal is given probation, he's relieved. He thinks, "I gotta toe the line now and report to my probation officer, but at least I'm not in jail!"—He's grateful for the lucky break. It's the same thing for the person who betrays his or her spouse. They have to be thankful they're granted a second chance, and the only way to show it is to be transparent.

On the other hand, if you are the victim, stop reminding your partner of the past and refrain from constantly being suspicious. Don't assume things or jump to conclusions. Deal with the present facts. If your partner doesn't change, you may then have to tell him or her that there won't be a third chance. But don't keep dredging up the past. If he or she is committed to changing, don't play detective, investigating what doesn't need to be investigated, or implying that he or she is still cheating on you. It's extremely annoying and frustrating if we're trying hard to change, while others make it obvious that they don't believe that we've changed at all.

It is common for someone who's been cheated on to start seeing things that don't exist. It's merely fear taking control. Even so, be rational. Paranoia and suspicion won't help. Be smart, make plans and be prepared for the possibility that the other person may not change—but leave the plan B "in the drawer" and only take it out if necessary. This way you'll already know what to do if the worst comes to the worst.

Bury the past and drive a steamroller over it 20 times, so you won't even know where to find it. Don't turn back to grieve over it or to spit on its grave. Forget it. Help your partner in the process of rebuilding the relationship. It takes teamwork. Is it hard? Yes, nobody said it would be easy, but it's the only way for you to start rebuilding broken trust.

Use this tool: In case of betrayal, lies or any breach of trust in the relationship if you've decided to give yourselves a second chance.

15. Sleep on it—This is not a contradiction to tool number 1, where we advised you not to sleep on an unresolved problem, leaving it for the next day. That tool is to help you deal with problems that have *already* *occurred*. This one teaches you to deal with stress *before* the problem happens. Many problems in marriage arise from stressful situations in one or both partners. If you stay tuned to detect the problem BEFORE it happens, you can avoid it.

Watch your spouse's body language, tone of voice and stress level. Give them enough space. People deal with stress differently. As a general rule, men need space and women need to talk. For sure, there are exceptions—there are women who also need silence and men who want to express their feelings. The important thing is to understand that if one is at a high level of irritability, it's useless trying to solve the problem right then and there.

This can also go along with the first rule: If the problem has already happened and you see that they are angry, it might be wiser to take a break to wait until he or she calms down. It's impossible to hold a conversation when people are acting on feelings and anger. This tool is similar to the "time out" rule in basketball. When the team starts losing points, the coach requests a time out, stops the game and gathers the players to give them new instructions. It's an effective strategy to interrupt the momentum of the opponent.

Remember that there is an opponent to your marriage too. Don't leave an entryway for the devil. If you keep nit-picking at your spouse when he or she is angry, then you're doing your opponent a favour. Take a break. Agree to talk about it later on.

Though this tool is called "Sleep on it," it doesn't necessarily mean that you have to sleep—though a good night's sleep is a great way to restore mental and emotional health. It could just as well be a 20-minute or one-hour break. The idea is to allow your partner to regain his strength and emotional balance.

Use this tool: To detect signs of stress in your partner or yourself and take a break or do whatever helps calm you both down before problems arise.

16. Script and rehearse it for next time—In marriage we rarely have new problems. Disagreements about money matters or raising the children don't come around only once. It's normal for couples to deal with recurring problems from time to time, so what do you do when an old problem pops up again? First, resolve the conflict immediately, using the 10 steps taught in chapter 6. Then ask yourself, "How can we prevent this from happening again?" or "What should we do if it does?" So as movie screenwriters plan what happens in the next scene, write your own "script" for the next time. What do you do when the same situation occurs? Decide what will happen, what each one's responsibilities will be, and make sure both of you agree on this. When a situation arises, both of you will know what to do, without losing your temper.

How does it work in practice? For example, a husband forgets his wedding anniversary. He's terrible with remembering dates to the irritation of his wife. And because he's forgetful, chances are that next year he'll forget it again. Some people are not really into remembering dates—it's a manufacturer's defect (as mentioned in tool 11). The couple must solve the problem of the wife's hurt feelings today, but also agree on how they'll handle this situation next time.

The wife can write it down on her husband's calendar at the beginning of the year (simple, right?), remind him well in advance, post notes around the house... "But it's not the same! He needs to *want* to remember and surprise me!"—she says. Understand one very important thing: Our high expectations can lead us to want our partners to be just like us, and to put the same importance on the things that we do, but it doesn't always work that way. It's necessary to adjust our expectations to avoid recurring problems. There's a big gap between the real and ideal worlds. The wider the gap, the greater the frustration, and more problems happen. Forget about the ideal world and deal with your reality. Even if your reality is not satisfying, it's what you've got, and what you have to work with to achieve better results.

This tool applies to all situations. Many argue about how to raise the kids—one is strict while the other is more flexible. It doesn't take long for the kids to figure this out, and start pitting one parent against the other to get their way. You both have to rehearse it for next time. Agree, for example, that the next time dad says no, and the child runs to mum in the hopes that she will override what dad just said, mum will instead stand by her husband's decision, even if she thinks that he was too harsh. You could discuss his judgment later when the kids aren't around to hear, but never let them see that you disagree with each other's decisions.

Another classic problem is money. You'd like your spouse to speak to you before spending so much money, but he or she doesn't. Now what? Some couples work it out and find common ground: "You can spend up to this amount, but anything above this, we need to talk over and decide together." This is how it's done. When a situation comes up, you already know how to deal with it, because you have a script.

Again, we go back to our business model. In business, you have to solve problems and prevent them from happening again, exactly what this tool is all about. In doing so, your problems will diminish considerably.

Use this tool: When you see a problem rearing its head from the grave while you moan, "Here we go again..."

17. Protect your evenings—Breaking news! Evenings are a time to unwind. If you usually discuss problems and air grievances at this time, when your partner comes home from work for example, you risk spoiling the mood for togetherness and intimacy—to put it bluntly, sex. One couple dealt with this by agreeing not to talk about problems after 8pm. It worked for them and you have to see what works for you. Just remember that if you're going to bed resenting each other or something that was said, you won't go to sleep as "one." This is the time of day to invest more in your relationship, as opposed to what many couples do who can't wait for their partners to get home to start complaining about the bills, or how the kids got into trouble with their teachers.

In The Love School "Lab" we had a couple with this problem. At dinnertime, she complained that he took too long to eat, but he asked her to give him some time because he wanted to relax and enjoy his meal. At one point, she said, "Why relax at dinner time? There's so much to get done. I still need to clean up. Who has time to relax?" Because of the many things to be done at home, this couple's nights are often chaotic. How could they invest in their intimacy if they can't relax during the only time of day they have together? Protecting your nights protects the hours leading up to intimacy. Many couples spend days, weeks and even months without having sexual intercourse because they neglect their evenings. You're hoping to have a good night together, but because of one word out of place at dinnertime, your plans go down the drain. Don't forget that sex begins in the mind. When you're not careful with your behaviour leading up to bedtime, you ruin the mood and blow your chances of a pleasant night between the sheets.

Use this: Every night and any other moment leading up to intimacy.

18. Rescue your partner—We can all feel overwhelmed at times. A wife may come home after a bad day at work and need to do a hundred household chores before she turns off the light to sleep. A caring husband will be sensitive to this and help ease the burden on her. He'll come to her rescue. "I'll take care of the groceries while you look at the kids' homework." "I'll fold the laundry and take the rubbish out while you make dinner." Picking up after yourself also helps! In the same way, a wife should be a helper to her husband and make sure that she steps in when he's overwhelmed. Love means caring for the other person.

Other examples of this tool could be, if she comes home stressed out and just wants to unwind, her husband could be sensitive to her exhaustion and order take-aways so that she won't need to cook dinner. She feels valued and cared for. And if her husband is stressed out and she gives him some space to unwind, she is helping as well. If you notice that your spouse isn't feeling or doing what he or she normally would, just do it yourself. Don't make a mountain out of a molehill. Be there for them when they need it the most. This is a tool for emergencies. Help each other when one of you is taking on more than they can handle. Remember the question: *What does my spouse need from me right now?* Is it emotional support, medical care, guidance, practical help, or just keeping them company?

Cristiane:

I never liked demanding that Renato help me with the housework. I've always been the old-fashioned-housewife type, who doesn't want her husband to worry about anything. But one day, I couldn't take it anymore. I was overloaded with responsibilities at home and at work. We lived with two other couples and when it was my turn to prepare lunch, I would cook for an army. Then I had to clean the kitchen and the rest of the house, besides preparing the afternoon snack and dinner... At the end of the day, I was beat! That was when I ended up in bed with a nasty bout of the flu.

I'll never forget what Renato did for me. He came to my rescue. He had always told me to hire someone to help with the housework twice a week, but because I didn't know anyone and was unsure if it would work out, I never tried. He called a cleaning service on his own, and signed a two-week contract, organising everything for me. I remember feeling so appreciated and valued by that simple gesture. He helped me when I needed it the most.

Housework is a subject that deserves special attention. Society has changed a lot, but the mentality of some people is still way behind. If you have constant arguments about the housework, make a list and agree on who is responsible for what. Who will take out the rubbish? Who will mow the lawn? Who will clean the bedroom? One of you? Both of you? The kids? Hire some help?

In a company, everyone knows who does what. Everything should be well defined. If everybody thinks that someone else will do it, then nobody does it. Set weekly, daily and monthly tasks and decide who will do what. If you have kids, they can help too, and the family will be a team caring for their own home. Put the list up on the refrigerator so nobody will forget it. It's a practical way to solve these problems.

Use this tool: Whenever you notice that your spouse is overloaded or unable to do their normal duties.

19. Don't make personal attacks—"You're a liar," "You're stupid," "You're stubborn." When you say things like that to your spouse, it's a sign that your relationship has descended to the lowest levels of disrespect—a trip it may not be able to come back from. Personal attacks mean that you've lost sight of who or what the real enemy is: the problem, rather than your partner. Don't go down that road, bring yourself back, and remember to focus on the problem. When you denigrate your spouse, you are cursing yourself, since it was you who chose to marry him!

Don't assume that your partner is lying. Two people can see the same scene and describe it in different ways. It doesn't mean that they are lying; they are just expressing their different points of view. Calling your spouse a liar for not agreeing with your version of the events can be a great injustice, so keep focused on the problem and don't attack their character. It's just not smart.

I cannot attack Cristiane as if she were the problem herself. I need to learn to separate her from the problem. I hate the problem, but still love Cristiane. You need to remember that you're friends and work together against the adversities that you are facing. You were both victims of a problem. You have now become its enemies, and both have the responsibility to figure out the solution, hand in hand.

Use this tool: In any conversation, especially when your partner annoys you.

20. Do not project—If you've had a bad experience with your mother or father, or in a previous relationship, it's very easy to unfairly project your insecurities of the past onto your present partner, e.g. A woman who was abused by her father can have unresolved resentments that cause her to overreact with all authority figures, even her husband. Or a man may have had a bad experience in his previous relationship and assume that his present wife is going to be unfaithful just like his ex.

If I was cheated on in the past, and I project my traumatic experiences onto my wife, even the smallest thing that resembles the behaviour of the other woman will cause me to feel jealous and suspicious, and my wife will never understand why. It's not her fault, but I'm already attacking her as if she had done the same thing. You project an image onto the other person as if he or she were at fault.

The example of a woman who was abused, and brings that trauma into her relationship, deserves a little more attention. She may be unable to have pleasure because of that abuse and feel disgusted with sexual intercourse. Her husband is not to blame, nor is the abused woman, but she is unable to deal with the situation. This problem has two sides: The projector and the screen that the image is being projected on to.

How can a traumatised person handle this situation? That's where the power of faith comes in. Psychologists and psychiatrists can certainly help, but human knowledge and medicine have their limits. Faith in God has no limits, and can heal the deepest wounds. God gives you the ability to forgive and even—literally—forget. He Himself uses that power for His own sake. It says in Isaiah 43:25, *"I, even I, am He who blots out your transgressions for* **My own sake; and I will not remember your sins."**

God, who has the ability to handle any situation, voluntarily decides not to remember our sins because He knows that it is no longer useful, practical information. If a person repents and decides to change his life, He forgets about it and does not hold onto it. If you can't do it alone, seek help from God. It's also worth remembering that your spouse is not to blame for what happened to you in the past, so be fair. If you are dealing with someone who is going through this situation, be patient. Be aware of their emotional baggage and be considerate instead of reacting negatively. Use your head to help those who are still trapped by their emotions.

Use this tool: Once you identify a traumatic event from the past as the root of a problem in your relationship.

21. Agree on how to raise the children: When there's no unified front on how to raise your children, you create a great deal of stress on your marriage, not to speak of confusing and frustrating your children. And <u>never</u> argue in front of the kids. If you disagree on something, discuss it in private. One of you can be very tough on the kids because of the way you were brought up, while the other may be more lenient, because of their past. Both methods may work, depending on the occasion, and you can make use of them both. Don't criticise your partner because he treats the children differently from you. Simply agree on how to do it in advance.

Children are children (and teenagers are basically overgrown children). They don't use their heads as much as their emotions because their minds are not yet fully developed. Unfortunately, your kids are not as emotionally mature as you'd like them to be. They'll get there, but until that happens, they need rules and discipline. They need boundaries, times to wake up, go to sleep, sit at the table and eat with the family, to stick to their curfew (for teens), and to know when to speak and when to remain silent. Children will always try to push your buttons and test their boundaries. Of course, it's great to give them freedom to discover new things, but it's not healthy to let them do whatever they want. Parents are responsible for establishing rules through interacting and talking without aggression. Remember tool 16: Script and rehearse it for next time. Children should not be given mixed messages.

If one of them starts to complain about either mum or dad, never criticise your spouse in front of your children. To prepare your children for the world, set boundaries and let them know about consequences and rewards. It's like driving a car. If you speed, you face the consequences of the law for your behaviour: A hefty fine. If you have to pay a speeding ticket, you'll be more careful next time and drive under the limit. Many parents don't bother to tell their kids about the consequences of their behaviour. I'm not talking about being too severe, but balanced—you don't want your children to be frightened. It's not about punishing them, but training them to help change their behaviour. It can be done when they know the consequences of bad behaviour and the rewards for good. So he got to school on time every day this week? Then he deserves to go to the movies over the weekend. That's life. If you do a great job, you expect your boss to recognise it, right? If this happens, you feel motivated to keep up the good work and do even better.

If your child is an adult and still lives with you, he can't be allowed to live in eternal teenager mode. He needs to contribute, help pay the bills, clean the house, and know the consequences of his choices. Unfortunately, many parents these days are raising bums because of the fear of being judged by a society that pits children against parents. They end up raising children who are totally unprepared for society. In the past, an 18-year-old guy was already a man, ready to take on his own responsibilities and care for his own family. Today, the majority of

YOUR SHIELD AGAINST DIVORCE

18-year-olds know nothing about life because their parents are letting society raise their children. You must establish a culture within your home—your own culture. Think about it, if there are rules even among gangsters (some of which are very strict), why can't you have rules too?

Use this tool: Daily, from the moment you decide to be parents, blending your parenting styles to arrive at an agreement on how to raise your children. Remember, preparing a human being for life is a big responsibility.

22. Remember that you're on the same team—What is more important, to be right or to be happy? For your marriage to do well or to prove yourself right? Individualistic people are terrible spouses. Couples have to learn to work as a team, because they are one. Put the wellbeing of your team first. You are always on each other's side. Sometimes you have to agree to disagree. A disagreement does not need to cause a fight. Stay united against the problems. Don't let them separate you. Never forget that the bottom line is that the whole team must win, and not just one of the players.

How does a team work? Basketball players dribble and pass the ball up through the team until it reaches someone close enough to pop it into the basket. Note that the personal goal of each player is, of course, to score as many points as he can to become the team's leading scorer. And yet, he's ready to give up any personal goals for the success of the team. At that moment, it's not important which player individually scores the points, but their strategy is to get the best-positioned player to dunk that basket and boost their score. And if the last player to get the ball misses, the rest of the team doesn't tear him down, because they're all committed to the game and know that they need to keep working together.

Another aspect of a team is to recognise the strengths and weaknesses of each player. Each player plays in a position where he performs best, and they all complement each other. Cristiane is a better organiser and get-it-done person than I, and a great accountant too. She handles the finances. I'm a better strategist and planner; I am more into details. So we both combine our forces for the good of our marriage.

Use this tool: From day one of your marriage, till death do you part. Especially when there is a disagreement, to prevent selfishness and problems from separating you.

23. Money issues are really about trust issues—Prenuptial agreements, separate bank accounts, keeping income/expenditure information from your partner, among others, are signs that there are serious trust issues in your relationship. Find out why you can't trust your partner or why she or he can't trust you with money—and deal with that issue. Money-related issues have been cited as the number one cause of divorce. Don't leave them unresolved.

We're not talking here about a couple's financial problems, but the problems between you that are caused by money. A husband thinks his wife spends too much or a wife complains that her husband can't save. You will argue until you're blue in the face if you don't deal with the root of the problem. How can I help my wife to learn to spend more wisely? Taking the credit card away from her won't solve the problem. If I take away her card, she'll still have that problem plus one more: She'll feel hurt because of my attitude. I should ask myself, "What do I really want?" I don't want to take the card from her, I want her to help me trust her more. What are the options for dealing with the root of this problem? Will we have to sit down and do a household budget together? Will I have to give her an allowance so she can develop this skill? I, being head of the home, have to help her.

On the other hand, if you admit you can't control your spending, or have an addiction that wastes your money, and you don't know how to control it, accept help from your spouse for the sake of the team. By working together to solve this situation, you will find the best solution to budgeting and eliminate the source of stress in your relationship.

Use this tool: If money issues have become a source of stress in your marriage. Seek out the root of distrust.

24. Don't cut each other off—When you have a disagreement, let your spouse explain his or her point of view before you start talking. Resist the temptation to defend yourself or counter-attack. This keeps the discussion on a rational level rather than on an emotional level. It is also important to focus on ONE POINT at a time. Do not finish talking about a subject until it has been resolved—only then move on to the next subject.

Here we have another problem of the two brains again. Men tend to do this naturally, talking out of that one particular box. Women already see all the connections to the problem. Soon, the argument has gone way off subject and has sunk to an irrational level. *What are we arguing about anyway?* Listen to your spouse first. Don't assume that you know what they're going to say before they've finished speaking. Don't think about your answer before you finish listening. It's not a competition, you don't have to defend yourself or win the debate. You must understand the problem rather than assume that you already do, and then talk. If you want to solve the problem, then let the other person speak.

Of course, this is not an excuse for those of you who can't stop talking and hog the conversation. I've seen plenty of couples where one is a born motormouth, and the other isn't. Arguments like these are annoying to watch when one dominates the conversation and the other can't even get a word in edgewise.

A good tip to avoid getting side-tracked is to write down the problems you want to solve. For example: *Our house needs urgent repairs and I've already told you about it several times.* Is that what you want to discuss? Then don't let the topic shift to your mother-in-law, the car, the dog, etc. Stay on that one subject only. Solve it, and then move on to the next.

Use this tool: Any time you feel like interrupting or taking over the conversation.

25. Have a sense of humour—Encourage each other's sense of humour. Laugh as much as possible. Have inside jokes that are private between the two of you. If you don't make each other laugh regularly and often, consider the alternative! One of the things I know that keeps our marriage healthy is our sense of humour. It's a way to relieve the tension and make life fun. Marriage is a lifelong journey—make sure your journey is exciting, not boring.

Cristiane and I don't have a busy social life, but even so, it's never boring when we're together, precisely because both of us share this fun sense of humour. We joke with each other and make funny, light-hearted comments on things happening around us throughout the day. Some couples don't like to be together. The times they spend alone together are so boring, they end up getting tired and give up on each other. But for us, our daily interactions are so much fun that we can't stand being apart for too long.

We play pranks and have jokes that we'll never share with anyone else, and we know that nobody else could enjoy them because they're our own inside jokes. By the way, ladies, one more tip: Men usually like to goof around and be funny. Some rarely talk about the same subjects their wives do, like relationships and their friends' lives and recent purchases. A husband can be extremely frustrated if he attempts to bring some fun into the relationship and his wife finds him silly and a nuisance (and even worse, when she tells him so). Then she complains that he watches too much television. What's fun about talking to someone who criticises you for being at ease and who forces you to be serious all the time? Though you have different senses of humour, you must learn to appreciate the funny side of your husband.

Being grumpy is not a sign of being responsible and mature. A recent survey by the accounting employment agency, Accountemps, showed that 79% of CFOs believe that good humour is essential for employees to do well in their companies. If it were a sign of irresponsibility or flippancy, do you really think experienced executives would take it into consideration when hiring?

The benefits of a good sense of humour go far beyond the workplace. An upbeat mood boosts the immune system, stimulates creativity, memory, and even helps reduce the sensation of pain, not to mention the increase in self-esteem! It's great when someone laughs with you. It creates bonds. Maybe your spouse would rather hang out with his friends because they laugh at his jokes! If you don't add anything to his or her times of fun, if you're a spoilsport and shrug off whatever your spouse or others have to say, why would anyone want to hang out with you?

Use this tool: As long as you breathe. Just be careful not to offend your partner with a joke that s/he does not appreciate or is said at inappropriate times.

26. Make sure you have his attention—You can include having *her* attention too, but this is a tool specifically for women. We mentioned earlier that due to the differences between men's and women's brains, women tend to multitask while men tend to do one thing at a time. So women, when you want to say something very important to your husbands, make sure their eyes are on you and have disconnected from any other activity! But be careful. This often means that you will have to interrupt and take his focus off what he is doing to focus on you. Choose the right time, speak gently—and still be prepared that you might have to remind your "clueless guy" again later about what you talked about, if it's really that important.

Use this tool: Whenever you need your other brain to register something important.

27. Keep romance alive—Marriage is not based on emotion, rather it's hard work and perseverance, but a little romance goes a long way. It's important for both partners in a marriage to constantly do special things for each other. If we're not careful, our jobs, the kids and other responsibilities and pressures will take up all our time. Make sure you have "just us" time. Taking work home on a regular basis, spending hours in front of the TV, allowing the kids to take all your time and attention are examples of behaviour that cause couples to grow apart. You need your "just us" time—make sure you plan for it.

Hollywood wants us to believe that romance has to be complicated, elaborate and expensive, but it doesn't. Romance can be defined as "doing something out of the ordinary that shows your love for the other person." It doesn't have to be a big thing, and it often isn't. Men, you may not consider yourself to be romantic, but it's not that hard. Just be spontaneous. You don't have to spend a lot of money to be romantic.

Here are some ideas: Call your wife in the middle of the day and ask her how she is. Leave a note, or a card like the ones you used to write when you were dating (you can put it under her pillow or by the sink, or tuck it into her suitcase when she's travelling). Giving flowers can seem like a cliché and insincere. Too many guys pick up a cheap bunch of carnations at the supermarket on the way home and think they're winning major points, but their wives see the lame attempt as just that —lame! If you get her flowers, find the ones you know she loves, ones with a special meaning to her. You can also turn off the phones, make popcorn, and rent a movie that she likes to watch while snuggling on the couch (no falling asleep during the movie—not romantic). Finally, be creative. Do something different, but simple, that shows you think of your spouse, even in the most mundane moments. Your homework is to do something romantic for your partner this weekend. Let's get going!

Use this tool: At least once or twice a month, and whenever the routine of married life turns boring. This is a maintenance tool. Surprise your spouse.

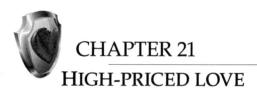

CHAPTER 21
HIGH-PRICED LOVE

A couple's 50th anniversary was approaching and they decided to celebrate. When asked about their secret to long-term harmony, the husband replied:

– You know the heel on a loaf of bread? Well, that's my favourite part, but every morning for 50 years I've given her the heel.

When his wife was asked the same question, she said:

– You know the heel on a loaf of bread? Well, I hate the heel! But for 50 years I've eaten the heel without complaining...

This small example reveals a big secret of what should be at the base of every marriage. In one word: Sacrifice. For 50 years he gave up what he liked out of love for her, and she gave up what she liked for him. Think of the foundation of a house or building. It keeps that structure standing. The same goes for sacrifice in marriage. When people look at a couple from the outside they don't see it, but their happiness is a direct result of the sacrifices they make for each other.

NINETEEN YEARS IN A COMA

Ever since hearing about this couple I've not been able to forget their example. For me, it's one of the best examples of what love truly is, the sacrificial love. Jan Grzebski was a Polish railroad worker. In 1988 he suffered a blow to the head while trying to connect two railroad cars together and fell into a coma. Doctors gave up on him, especially after discovering he had a brain tumour. Their opinion was that he would never recover or even survive much longer. Gertruda Grzebska, Jan's wife, ignored those words of defeat and decided to take him home and care for him on her own.

Still in a coma, Jan could not speak, walk, communicate or interact in any way. They no longer had a relationship. The strong husband who had always been at her side was now a baby, totally dependent on her as his caregiver. She finished raising their children on her own, while struggling to keep her husband alive. He could only do the most basic activities such as breathing, swallowing and opening and closing his eyes. And yet she would get extremely angry whenever anyone suggested euthanasia (arguing that it would "end that suffering") because she believed the right thing was to give him a chance to recover. Every day Gertruda spoke to her husband as though he could hear her and kept turning him so he didn't develop bedsores—common in bedridden patients which can lead to deadly infections. The children grew up, got married and gave them grandchildren. Gertruda took her husband to all major family get-togethers as if he were able to participate.

Tireless Gertruda received her reward in 2007. After 19 years in a coma, Jan finally awakened at the age of 65. Doctors credited his recovery to his wife, who chose the hardest path. Jan had an even stronger connection with her now because he remembered that she was at his side when he most needed her. She did what was right and best for him, giving up her own life to take care of her husband, without demanding anything in return. She believed even when doctors didn't. She waited, persisted... and was rewarded.

During the coma, Gertruda described her husband as "a living corpse", yet she still remained by his side. There were no emotions in what she did, or romance, it was pure sacrifice, true love—but can you think of anything more romantic? No love story is more beautiful than those that involve sacrificial love. Gertruda received a well-deserved medal of honour from the president of Poland for her dedication and sacrifice, reinforcing how rare it is to find this kind of love nowadays.

Looking at the harsh reality that Gertruda endured for 19 years, the inevitable questions are: What would you have done in her place? What do you make of the problems you are facing in *your* marriage? Will you give up on your spouse?

Only sacrificial love overcomes all things. It's a high-priced, genuine love. Beware of cheap imitations.

LOSE TO WIN

Sacrifice is the way to put everything we've taught you throughout this book into practice. In fact, every successful person is familiar with the concept of sacrifice. In any area of life, when a person conquers something of great value, performs great deeds or obtains victories, they will have had to cross the bridge of sacrifice. This is the shortest path to success. But, of course, it is not the easiest.

What is sacrifice? Let's say it's extremely cold, I have two coats and the person next to me is shivering. I give him one coat and keep the other one. This would not be a sacrifice; it would simply be giving. But if I only have one coat and give that coat to that other person, now I'm sacrificing. Sacrifice is giving up something now because you are certain that you will gain something of much greater value in the future. At times, this thing of greater value is your clear conscience, knowing that you did the right thing, not what you felt like doing. This is what Gertruda did.

True love is marked by sacrifice. It's expensive. As we've already mentioned, love is not an emotion. It includes feelings, but is not defined by them. The world mixes love with emotions in a recipe that's pretty indigestible: Measure out the word "love", the desire to be together, jealousy, greed, sexual desire... mix them all together, then heat it up with music, movies, and art, and then sell it to people as "love". It's not. It's counterfeit. The combination of two things is what defines love:

1. Doing what is right for the other person. I have to be fair to the person I love. I have to do right by her, no matter what I do or do not feel, think or do not think, or how much it's going to cost.

2. Sacrifice. If your love is simply a good feeling, it will not survive the storms. The only love that outlasts any problem is a love that's not based on feelings, but on sacrifice. Those who say "our love ran out" do not know what love is. True love never ends.

The selfishness of present day couples blocks them from putting this concept into practice, telling them that they'll get hurt when they sacrifice. But those who've chosen to walk the path of true love have no regrets.

I don't want you to equate marriage with suffering or carrying a heavy cross for all eternity. Sacrifice is not an end in itself, it's simply a means of achieving something greater. It is like a person who applies for a challenging new job that pays three times his current salary. If he doesn't sacrifice his free time to study, take a course or brush up on his skills, he can't expect to get that job. Start sacrificing for your marriage and you'll have a wonderful relationship of peace, understanding, companionship and loyalty... one that more than makes up for all the suffering you had to go through in the beginning. Without a doubt you'd do it all over again after seeing the results. Try it.

You may ask, "But aren't there limits? What if my spouse never gives back, am I stuck with him for the rest of my life?"

Obviously some people don't want another person's love. Some even reject God's love. So, having a relationship with these people is impossible. Not even God forces people to love or follow Him. He sacrificed for everyone, but not everyone accepts His sacrifice or the conditions they need to meet to have a relationship with Him.

Love should be unconditional when it comes to understanding your partner's weaknesses. But when it comes to a relationship or marriage, it should never be unconditional. For two people to live together, certain prerequisites must be met. I love my wife, but if she cheats on me, I don't see how I could possibly continue a relationship with her. I know she feels the same way about me. Faithfulness is a prerequisite for our marriage to work. Would I give her another chance if there were sincere repentance? Maybe. Every case is different, and everyone has his own faith and limitations. But one thing is certain: A good relationship requires involvement from both parties. If the other person doesn't want you, then your sacrifice may be better spent on someone else.

HOW DO WE APPLY THIS TO MARRIAGE?

I am going to list some examples (there are many more) of sacrifice in marriage so you can better understand when and how this applies:

The sacrifice of communication—I had to learn to communicate more with Cristiane. I was not used to coming over to her and having a conversation. I was frequently tired and enjoyed being quiet. I would communicate in one-word sentences. Out of love, I sacrificed this behaviour and began to answer her questions. Even now when she asks me questions, I find that I have to force myself to answer her because I don't always feel like talking, I see no sense in talking about certain things, but I think to myself: What I feel doesn't matter. I'm going to do what's important to her. When a husband is the quiet-type and his wife is very talkative, it's a sacrifice for him to be talkative with his wife. On the other hand, nobody can stand a wife who talks too much, is demanding, imposing and pushy. Her husband will find her to be a much nicer person if she makes the sacrifice to slow down and be less demanding. If both do this, they'll create a healthy balance. If only one does it, only half of the problem will be solved... but the other half will be positively affected and the other half of the problem will sooner or later be solved also.

The sacrifice of humility—This happens when you swallow your pride, give in and admit that your partner is right. This is a sacrifice because it hurts, but sacrificing your pride and admitting your mistakes mean that you're not feeding a hard heart.

Sacrificing your free time—It's a sacrifice when your wife likes to go out and you take her out simply to please her, or when your husband doesn't like to go out and you stay home with him and avoid complaining about it. Your husband loves football, but you can't understand what is so interesting about a bunch of men chasing a ball. And yet you sit next to him and try to learn how to enjoy it, seeing it through his eyes because it's important to him. Just seeing your spouse happy will make it fun for you.

The sacrifice of sex—When you look at sex in a selfish way and refuse to sacrifice during it, your goal is your own pleasure, nothing more. When you learn how to sacrifice, you'll be able to put your partner's pleasure above yours. Then neither of you will ever feel ignored because your goal is to please the other person and you'll not be satisfied until he or she is. Mutual pleasure can only be found through sacrifice.

The sacrifice of irritability—There are times when we need to simply ignore annoying habits. Think about it: Compared to all the other positive aspects of the relationship, that habit is totally insignificant. You won't make a big deal out of a small thing.

The sacrifice of emotions—This might be one of the greatest sacrifices because it has to do with the heart. Knee-jerk reactions and emotion cause couples to hurt each other, feed on each other's anger and then sleep in separate rooms. We have to sacrifice our emotional instincts that lead us to act before we think. I will not allow my emotions to persuade me to insult my wife. I have to respect her. Neither will I annoy her with endless complaints, which lead to pointless and unnecessary arguments. Cristiane stopped complaining to me and began complaining to God, asking Him to change my behaviour. She sacrificed her emotions and relied on God.

The sacrifice of goals—When your personal goals exclude your marriage, it is often necessary to sacrifice them. Whenever we place our personal goals above our relationship, it damages it. This is why many celebrity marriages end in divorce. If your career is more of a priority than your marriage, your partner will feel that he or she is simply an add-on to your life. It's hard to bear a situation like this for very long. Both of you should sacrifice your personal goals and find common ones.

The sacrifice of friendships—If a friend has a negative influence on your marriage, or makes your spouse feel uncomfortable or suspicious, you should sacrifice that friend for your marriage. Friends of the opposite sex or relatives who cause jealousy should be kept at a distance.

FORGIVENESS: THE GREATEST OF ALL SACRIFICES

If your spouse has caused you a lot of pain and disappointment, and you want to move forward in the relationship, you need to press the "reset" button. When your computer crashes, restarting it will frequently take care of the problem. Likewise, for your marriage to work you have to press the reset button by forgiving.

We do not *feel* like forgiving. What we feel like doing is punishing the other person. We're tempted to think that forgiveness means that the other person will never suffer the consequences of their actions. And so we hold a grudge as a way of exacting revenge. There is a saying: Refusing to forgive is like drinking rat poison and waiting for the rat to die. Think about it, the rat's not going to die! You drank the poison; you're going to die. The rat's going to be free, running back and forth, up to no good and gnawing at everything he comes across. Who loses in this scenario?

Bitterness enslaves. It's a burden that is not consistent with intelligence. Why lug around an unnecessary burden? The other person has already gotten over the past and is looking ahead, but you're at a standstill obsessing over the past. Forgive, not because the other person deserves it, but because you don't want to be burdened with it. Bitterness is emotional rubbish. When you feed bitterness, you're eating rubbish. It's as if you're eating rotten food, walking around with a backpack of rancid food that you plan to eat for dinner, and whenever anyone tells you to get rid of it, you tighten your grip.

I know exactly what this feels like. I was bitter toward a person in my family who was partially responsible for my parents' separation. As a teen I made a promise to myself to pay this person back for what she had done. When I began attending church and heard the pastor say that we had to forgive our enemies, my first thought was: *You don't know the person who destroyed my family. It's easy for you to say because you don't know what I went through.* Maybe this is what's going through your mind as you read about forgiveness. I didn't understand it at first, but over time I realised that she was not being hurt by my bitterness. I was being hurt. When I understood that I needed to forgive for my own good, I got interested in finding out how this could be done, since I really didn't feel like doing it.

SO... HOW DOES A PERSON FORGIVE?

The first thing to know about forgiveness is that it's not a feeling; it's a decision. Deciding to forgive was not difficult, since I understood it was the right thing to do. I just needed the ability to move on. The second step was to start praying for her. Many who continue to carry emotional rubbish claim that they pray for their enemies, yet what they say in their prayers doesn't help. You can't expect to get rid of bitterness when you pray: *Lord, make John pay for what he did.* That's not praying for your enemies! That prayer is anger that God will not listen to. The Bible tells us to bless those who persecute us[21]... *Bless and do not curse.* That's how we should pray.

At first my prayers were insincere. I would start off praying for her, asking God to bless her, but what I really wanted Him to do was strike her in the head with a lightning bolt. Ignoring my desire to see her torn into a million pieces, I continued to pray. Over time, the stone that had been my heart shattered and I started seeing her in a different light. Prayer helped me change the way I looked at her. That's when I took the third step: I began to look forward. I realised that I had to be practical. Looking back was not smart. What was done was done. If she needed to pay for what she had done, that would be God's problem; I had nothing to do with it. I also realised that I had many flaws and had no right to demand perfection from her, because I wasn't perfect either. If God, who is perfect, looked at me with the same severity that I looked at her, I would be completely lost! But if I welcomed His forgiveness, how could I not forgive as well? *And forgive us our debts as we forgive our debtors[22].* When you do not forgive, you can't even pray The Lord's Prayer. Have you thought about it that way? It's unfair for me to want something that I'm not willing to give.

This is the difference between genuine and emotional love. Our hearts are the centre of our emotions and will always insist on doing what they feel like doing rather than what needs to be done. You may

---

[21] Romans 12:14
[22] Matthew 6:12

know that the right thing to do is talk to your spouse, but you may not feel like doing it. Your heart will quickly come up with an excuse: *Why do I have to talk to him? He's the one who was wrong!* But when we use our heads, take charge of our hearts, and refuse to live by emotions, we'll do the right thing even when it's not what we want to do.

It's a constant war. I can't predict what I'm about to feel. No one has control over that. Emotions come like waves. But I can control my head; I can determine what I think and how I react to a feeling. Whenever my heart is using my own emotions against me, I have to use my intelligence.

Does this sound impossible? You do this every morning, especially Monday mornings. You don't feel like getting out of bed. You want more sleep. You press the snooze button and are rewarded with an extra five minutes of dreamland. But when the alarm goes off again, your head says: *You can't miss work. You can't be late again. Get up and go to work.* So you get up and drag yourself to the bathroom against your own will. If needed, you even jump into the shower before the water's heated up just to show your heart who's the boss. Now in retreat, it gives up insisting and you're able to eat breakfast and go to work. If you didn't do this, you wouldn't have a job, right? This is how to win the battles in your marriage. Yes, it's a sacrifice, but it's absolutely doable. Everything that's really nice is expensive.

TASK:

What sacrifices do you need to start making, or continue making, for your relationship?

/BulletproofMarriage

Post: I don't want cheap love and so I've decided to sacrifice. #Bulletproofmarriage

@BulletproofMate

Tweet: I don't want cheap love and so I've decided to sacrifice. #BulletproofMarriage @BulletproofMate

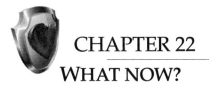

CHAPTER 22
WHAT NOW?

We truly hope that you've woken up to the fact that marriage in the 21st century is not what it used to be. We're living in a new world, surrounded by a culture of apathy, and a new set of threats that did not exist only a number of years ago. For those who still want to get married and stay married, bulletproofing your relationship is no longer a luxury, it's a necessity.

What we've done up to this point in this book is exactly the opposite of what the world is doing. While the world talks about being liberal, progressive, modern and sleeping around—we've gone right back to the beginning of all things, to the Garden of Eden, and traced the footsteps of men and women right up to the present time. We've covered the essence of marriage, what works, that love is marked by what we do, not by how we feel, the curses affecting men and women, how they affect their relationship, and how to deal with them. We also learned about the fundamental differences between the sexes and their inherent conflicts. We learned to identify the root of a problem and solve it by using reason instead of emotion. We spoke about dozens of practical tools that can be applied to your marriage on a daily basis, to solve and prevent problems.

You learned a little about Cristiane and me, and we hope that our struggles and experiences have in some way helped you to better understand your own marriage. We tried to give you a realistic idea of what marriage is, revealing its difficulties but also its joys and beauty. A happy marriage takes work, yes—but the payoff is worth all the effort! We want to raise the flag of true love, challenge the myths and misinformation that plague today's relationships, and show that you can be married and very happy. We honestly believe that only happily married couples experience complete happiness. This is why we were created. It is possible. Do not let anyone tell you otherwise.

Cristiane and I do not consider ourselves "lucky". Our happy marriage is the result of our decisions, which often went against our feelings, and the practice of spiritual intelligence, which is obedience to the advice of God. If we had not done this, and continued doing what we had done in the beginning, we would be another statistic. Anyone— including you—who puts this advice into practice, can have a happy marriage. This should not be taken lightly. We are here because we've lived out our faith. Intelligence refuses to believe that a successful love life is possible without the True Love—God. Everything you want to accomplish in life, not only in your marriage, is possible through faith in Him—even the answers you have not found in this book. And so, in response to the question "What now?" we would advise:

Seek a close relationship with the God of the Bible through the Lord Jesus. He doesn't want you to become religious, but rather to develop a relationship with Him.

Plus, we are absolutely certain that the principles and practical lessons you learned in this book, work. They are not always easy to put into practice, but they work. Difficult is not the same as impossible, and just because there may be a delay in seeing results, that does not mean they won't come. Be patient and persistent. Don't expect a complete

YOUR SHIELD AGAINST DIVORCE

change within a matter of days, and don't demand that of your partner. Start with a first step and continue working at it.

We think you should focus on some key points: One, two or three main points that touched you the most, and that you know require urgent attention. Work on these points until they become a part of your life. Then go back to the other chapters and work on other areas. It's like changing your eating habits. You may want to lose weight, but you know that you can't drastically cut down your calories and starve because that won't work. But if you change your diet gradually and exercise more often, the result will come naturally and it'll be permanent. Stay focused on change and continuous effort, and you'll reach your goal. Do not give up. As the saying goes, a thousand-mile journey begins with a single step. The results will come with practice.

Cristiane and I want to be a positive influence in your life and would like to suggest some steps that can bring results for your relationship and help others. Here they are:

1. Review the sections of this book that caught your attention, or that you feel are most needed. You'll be surprised by how much this will help you to absorb and retain the most important points. It will help you remember what you learned and how to act in the future.

2. If you did not complete all of the tasks, there's still time. Go back and work on them. Do not underestimate the power of implementing them. Whether you feel like it or not, do it!

3. Keep in touch with us through our websites and blogs. We would love to receive your feedback and continue to help you. Leave a comment, watch our videos, tell us your experiences. This is also how you can stay informed of what we're up to, our calendar of events around the world:

- Blogs: renatocardoso.com and cristianecardoso.com
- Facebook: fb.com/BulletproofMarriage
- Twitter: @BulletproofMate; Renato @brcardoso; Cristiane @cris-cardoso
- E-mail: book@bulletproofmarriage.org

4. Do something nice for someone else by giving him or her a copy of this book. If someone you know is about to get married and needs to learn to do things the right way, get them a copy. If you know someone who's married and needs to bulletproof their relationship give them this book as a present. They will thank you and will most probably never forget you.

5. We suggest that you keep your copy of this book and read it again in six months. Change takes time and requires persistence. So, go to your calendar now and make this note six months from today: "Reread Bulletproof Marriage book." Those who do this will see much greater results.

Happy bulletproof marriage!
Renato & Cristiane Cardoso

ACKNOWLEDGEMENTS

First of all, to the inventor of marriage: God. To the casual observer, making men and women so different from each other and getting them to live together may seem like a bad joke. But God always knows what He's doing. We're grateful to Him also for the gift that we've found in each other. Renato wouldn't be Renato without Cristiane, who wouldn't be Cristiane without Renato. It's hard to explain.

We're thankful for all the problems we went through in our marriage, which were tough but good teachers.

To Bishop Edir Macedo and Ester, perhaps the happiest and most solid couple we know. No other couple has positively influenced us more than you. Thank you for the teachings, many of which are all over this book.

To David and Evelyn Higginbotham, who helped us develop the marriage course in Texas, which gave birth to this book. Your always-excellent insights, friendship, servant attitude, the translation work you did here... where should we stop?

And to all our dedicated Bulletproof Marriage team, supporters and students of The Love School. You all share in our success. Celebrate with us!

Renato & Cristiane Cardoso

BIBLIOGRAPHY

Introduction

"Marriage and Divorce Statistics." *epp.eurostat.ec.europa.eu*. Eurostat European Commission, 8 Jan. 2013. Web. 12 Aug. 2013. http://goo.gl/6ElGsG

"Most Babies Born out of Marriage by 2016, Trend Suggests." *bbc.co.uk*. BBC, 11 July 2013. Web. 12 Aug. 2013. http://goo.gl/u88WTF

Chapter 1

Leff, Alex. "'Til 2013 Do Us Part? Mexico Mulls 2-year Marriage." Reuters. N.p., 29 Sept. 2011. Web. 12 Aug. 2013. http://reut.rs/1ctnzda

DeParle, Jason, and Sabrina Tavernise. "For Women Under 30, Most Births Occur Outside Marriage." Nytimes.com. The New York Times, 17 Feb. 2012. Web. 12 Aug. 2013. http://goo.gl/20i3q

Wiley-Blackwell. "Do children need both a mother and a father?" ScienceDaily. 28 January 2010. Web. 12 Aug. 2013. http://goo.gl/ZPeYp

Paul, Pamela. "Are Fathers Necessary?" The Atlantic. Atlantic Media, 8 June 2010. Web. 12 Aug. 2013. http://goo.gl/frSb4w

Stevens, John. "The Facebook Divorces: Social Network Site Is Cited in 'a THIRD of Splits'" Mail Online. Associated Newspapers Ltd, 30 Dec. 2011. Web. 12 Aug. 2013. http://goo.gl/D8VZC

Gardner, David. "The Marriage Killer: One in Five American Divorces Now Involve Facebook." Mail Online. Associated Newspapers Ltd, 2 Dec. 2010. Web. 12 Aug. 2013. http://goo.gl/qOUF2

"Internet Pornography Statistics" – TopTenReviews. TechMedia Network, n.d. Web. 12 Aug. 2013. http://goo.gl/sVnAk

"Statistics on Pornography, Sexual Addiction and Online Perpetrators." And Their Effects on Children, Pastors and Churches. TechMission, n.d. Web. 12 Aug. 2013. http://goo.gl/GUqHql

"ChristiaNet Poll Finds That Evangelicals Are Addicted to Porn." Marketwire. N.p., 7 Aug. 2006. Web. 12 Aug. 2013. http://goo.gl/OKfAYB

"Wounded Clergy: Ministers Are Not Immune To Compulsive Sexual Behavior!" Hopeandfreedom.com. Hope & Freedom Counseling Services, n.d. Web. 12 Aug. 2013. http://goo.gl/5FuKoQ

Sampaio, Rafael, and Luisa Ferreira. "Women are the majority in universities around the world" R7.com. Record TV Network, 26 Nov. 2010. Web. 12 Aug. 2013. http://goo.gl/FDvS8b

Cardoso, Rodrigo, and Carina Rabelo. "Women Are Cheating More." ISTOÉ – Independente. Terra.com, n.d. Web. 12 Aug. 2013. http://goo.gl/2xMtTl

"Pornography Statistics." *Familysafemedia.com*. Family Safe Media, n.d. Web. 12 Aug. 2013. http://goo.gl/n0i7o8

Chapter 2
Covey, Stephen. "Part 1." *The 7 Habits of Highly Effective People*. London: Simon & Schuster, 1999. Print.

Chapter 4
Fahmy, Miral. "In Love? It's Not Enough to Keep a Marriage, Study Finds." Reuters.com. Ed. Nick Macfie. Reuters, 14 July 2009. Web. 12 Aug. 2013. http://goo.gl/hk2x1Z

The Barna Group. "New Marriage and Divorce Statistics Released." *Barna.org*. The Barna Group, 31 Mar. 2008. Web. 12 Aug. 2013. http://goo.gl/nxv3Ca

Chapter 6
"5 Whys." *Wikipedia.org*. Ed. Wikipedia. Wikipedia, n.d. Web. 12 Aug. 2013. http://goo.gl/SPT3vd

Chapter 7
Seckel, Al, and John Edwards. "Franklin's Unholy Lightning Rod." *Evolvefish.com*. Evolvefish, n.d. Web. 12 Aug. 2013. http://goo.gl/yh8Svq

Chapter 8
"Soulmate." *Wikipedia.org*. Wikipedia, n.d. Web. 12 Aug. 2013. http://goo.gl/QerMuB

Chapter 15
Gray, John, Dr. "The Male vs. the Female Brain." *Thirdage.com*. Thirdage, 27 Apr. 2007. Web. 12 Aug. 2013. http://goo.gl/Z4c02Z

Brainfacts.org. Brain Facts – A Public Information Initiative of The Kavli Foundation, the Gatsby Charitable Foundation, and the Society for Neuroscience, n.d. Web. 12 Aug. 2013. http://goo.gl/TlwajV

Brizendine, Louann. *The Female Brain*. New York: Morgan Road, 2006. Print.

Gungor, Mark. *Laugh Your Way to a Better Marriage: Unlocking the Secrets to Life, Love, and Marriage*. New York: Atria, 2008. Print.

Chapter 16
hooks, bell. *Feminist Theory*. Cambridge, MA: South End, 2000. 26. Print.

Brasil.gov.br. "1977 Divorce Law." *Brasil.gov.br*. Jornal Do Brasil, n.d. Web. 12 Aug. 2013. http://goo.gl/00NnRD (Divorce & Feminism)

Chapter 17
Merriam-Webster Online Dictionary. "Husband." *Merriam-webster.com*. Merriam-Webster Online, n.d. Web. 12 Aug. 2013. http://goo.gl/2UGfzn

Chapter 20
"Avoid Divorce with 5:1 Ratio." *Marriagegems.com*. Marriage Gems, 25 July 2011. Web. 12 Aug. 2013. http://goo.gl/tmaANL

"Accountemps Survey: Executives Say Humor Is Key Part of Cultural Fit." *Accountemps.com*. Accountemps, 31 Jan. 2012. Web. 12 Aug. 2013. http://goo.gl/gAnqTR

8 — manus.

07-42 94 28 9 24

A world of different

BoB. (fart-may

by—   cLiy